KEEP
YOUR KIDS
CATHOLIC

"*Keep Your Kids Catholic* is a vigorous, inviting work by one of the best catechists around. Marc Cardaronella is on target as usual, bringing vitality, precision, and inspiration to a superbly written book that is equal parts field guide, spiritual retreat, and personal witness. Parents and grandparents, do not miss this exceptional resource!"

Lisa Mladinich
Catholic author and creator of Amazing Catechists

"In *Keep Your Kids Catholic*, Marc Cardaronella offers a wellspring of practical guidance from a very personal perspective, sharing his own spiritual journey and walking with your family as mentor and coach. A fantastic guidebook for any domestic church!"

Lisa M. Hendey
Founder of *CatholicMom.com* and author of *The Grace of Yes*

"Positive and strong Catholic parenting that dares to actively and intentionally raise kids in the faith is one tough mission and Marc Cardaronella offers parents a plan of committed action for getting our lives and our homes in order. This is straight talk from a tough-guy Navy pilot turned top-gun Catholic catechist. His love of the faith is infectious!"

Pat Gohn
Catholic writer, speaker, and author of *Blessed, Beautiful, and Bodacious*

"A stunning call to arms for Catholic families. Any parent or grandparent who wishes to see their children grow up to be practicing Catholics will find inspiration in this book. Pastors, principals, directors of religious education, teachers, and catechists will rejoice in providing this new resource to the families they serve because it is just the book they have been waiting for."

Jared Dees
Author of *To Heal, Proclaim, and Teach* and creator of *TheReligionTeacher.com*

KEEP
YOUR KIDS
CATHOLIC

SHARING YOUR FAITH
AND MAKING IT STICK

MARC CARDARONELLA

FOREWORD BY SCOTT HAHN, AUTHOR OF *ANGELS AND SAINTS*

Founded in 1865, Ave Maria Press is a ministry of the United States Province of Holy Cross.

www.avemariapress.com

Paperback: ISBN-13 978-1-59471-605-8

E-book: ISBN-13 978-1-59471-606-5

Cover and text design by Katherine J. Ross.

Cover image © Gettyimages.com.

Printed and bound in the United States of America.

Library of Congress Cataloging-in-Publication Data
Names: Cardaronella, Marc, author.
Title: Keep your kids Catholic : sharing your faith and making it stick /
    Marc Cardaronella.
Description: Notre Dame, Indiana : Ave Maria Press, 2016. | Includes
    bibliographical references.
Identifiers: LCCN 2016000581 (print) | LCCN 2016002151 (ebook) | ISBN
    9781594716058 | ISBN 1594716056 | ISBN 9781594716065 () | ISBN 1594716064 ()
Subjects: LCSH: Christian education of children. | Catholic
    Church--Doctrines. | Catholic Church--Education.
Classification: LCC BV1471.3 .C37 2016 (print) | LCC BV1471.3 (ebook) | DDC
    248.8/45088282--dc23
LC record available at http://lccn.loc.gov/2016000581

CONTENTS

FOREWORD

Several popes in succession have urged us to take up the task of a New Evangelization. The call originated with Blessed Paul VI, St. John Paul II made it a major theme of his papacy, and Benedict XVI worked it out theologically and practically for us. But Pope Francis told us where the primary work needs to be done: evangelization has to begin at home, with the family.

Our first mission is to the people God has placed in closest proximity to us. We can dream all we want about mission trips to faraway lands. We can plan strategic conversations with non-Catholic neighbors and coworkers. We can volunteer time at soup kitchens and shelters. But if we succeed in doing all those things, yet leave our family wanting, we will actually have failed.

Marc Cardaronella knows this; he wants us to succeed where God wants us to succeed, and he knows what works. His is not a fancy program that costs hundreds of dollars. It's an exhortation to us to make use of basic equipment that comes, free of charge, with the life of the Church.

What our families need is to live out the Catholic faith in all its biblical, ritual, traditional, devotional richness. For decades, I have been touring the world, speaking, writing books, teaching, and otherwise working full-time in the Catholic apostolate. Yet I can say truthfully that nothing for me has been more satisfying than the time I spent in prayer and study with my children. It's gratifying now to see them, all grown up, doing the same with their children.

I've often said that if Catholic couples simply allow their lives to be molded by the grace of the Sacrament of Matrimony, we'd change the world in forty years. Evangelization would happen, from the home outward. This book will teach you how to make that happen. And you will find the task irresistibly enjoyable.

Scott Hahn
Author of *Angels and Saints*

PREFACE

I have to be one of the most unlikely Christian parents ever. If I can do this, so can you.

I dropped out of religious education right after my Confirmation at thirteen. For twenty years, I didn't practice the Catholic faith—or any faith. I never went to church on Sundays, and even though we were married in the Catholic Church, my wife and I swore we would never have kids. And yet, here I am. I came back to the Church when I was thirty-three, and my whole life turned upside down. Now I'm hopelessly, faithfully Catholic and on a quest to make sure my two boys grow up in the bosom of the Catholic faith and stay there. I would like to help you do that with your children, too.

I'm not an expert in child psychology, behavioral therapy, or family counseling. I didn't major in family studies, and I haven't conducted a major study of what parenting styles produce vocations to the priesthood. I'm just a father and a professional religious educator. I work for the Catholic diocese in Kansas City, Missouri, and teach the Catholic faith for a living. I study evangelization strategies for professional development, research Internet marketing and relational psychology as a hobby, and try things out with my own kids to figure out what works. That's where this book comes from.

My first job working for the Catholic Church was as a parish director of religious education. Word got around that I had come back to the Church as an adult after having been away for some years, and older couples began approaching me about their adult children who had become Protestant or just walked away from

ix

Christianity altogether. They wanted to know what they could say to bring their kids back to the Catholic Church. I told them what brought me back to the Church and gave them some strategies, but I don't think they were successful. It was just too late. Adult children don't usually listen to their parents about faith. I know I didn't.

But those conversations stuck with me. Hearing the regret in their voices, I felt a calling to help parents nurture and grow the Catholic Christian faith in their children. I wanted to help the children, too, so that they wouldn't fall away from the Church as I did. It saddens me to realize how much wisdom I missed without the Church's guidance in my teen and young adult years. As I delved into the topic, my research quickly made it clear that the best place to plant strong childhood faith is in the family. Equipping families to hand on the Catholic faith became my passion.

Most parents don't think about their children's religious needs when the kids are young. It's all they can do to take care of the physical and emotional needs of infants and toddlers. Then, when their kids are old enough to go to school, parents assume that parish religious education programs or Catholic schools will teach them what they need to know for a lifetime of Catholic practice. However, there's a core component of faith formation that's difficult to instill within a parish program or Catholic school setting, one that would ideally begin long before a child reaches school age and that is uniquely suited to cultivation within families. What I'm talking about is an active relationship with Christ that continues to mature throughout life.

The fostering of a personal relationship with Christ is a huge gap in many religious education programs today. It's not hard to grasp that this lacking leads to the startling statistic from the Center for Applied Research in the Apostolate (CARA) that roughly 53 percent of Catholics leaving the Church in the early years of this century do so before the age of twenty-one.[1] Religious education methods from fifty or sixty years ago simply aren't working now. Millennials don't accept Church doctrine and authority just because it's what they're supposed to do. They need more. They need reasons to believe and causes to believe in, and many parishes fail to offer either to them.

Until the middle of the twentieth century, faith development occurred within the family. Devout parents passed down their religious beliefs, practices, and devotions within the context of a family life centered in the home. Today, that parental privilege and responsibility has largely been handed over to the parish or school. It's not entirely the fault of parents. For much of the last century, that's what the Church asked of parents. Too often, the message parishes communicated was "Bring your children to us. We're the experts. Don't worry, we'll teach them what they need to know and give them the sacraments, and they'll be set." We know better now. Too many kids have grown up and are growing up with little knowledge about what the Church teaches but without the one thing they need to sustain them for a lifetime—faith and an intimate relationship with God.

We have to take that back, and the family is still the place to do it. St. John Paul II once wrote, "The future of humanity passes by way of the family."[2] We all know he's right, that the family is the battleground for the future of faith in the Catholic Church. I truly believe there's hope. Parents can and must reclaim their rightful place as the first proclaimers of the Gospel to their children.

This book is perhaps a departure from most books on Christian parenting. There's a lot of emphasis on you, the parent: instead of simply telling you what to do for your children, I stress the importance of your own spiritual growth. I show you how to develop your faith life and maintain it. You are your children's primary educator in the faith; whether you ever speak a word about religion to them or not, you're teaching them. By what you say and what you don't say, by what you do and what you don't do, you're teaching them. That may not be comforting to you—I know it's not to me. But it's true. Your actions are an education for your children. How you live your life will significantly influence who and what they become. So if you want them to be religious, you need to be religious yourself.

This book offers some ideas for how you and your children can grow in faith together. While I cannot say with 100 percent certainty that these strategies will give your children an unshakable faith, I believe they will make a significant difference. But people are unpredictable—your children may still reject the Catholic faith even after you diligently carry out everything in this book. Of one thing I'm certain: the strategies in this book work far better than doing nothing. I draw on my catechetical training and incorporate lessons learned through twelve years of working with people joining the Catholic Church as adults. I also glean wisdom from my own parenting in our secular world and from the testimonies of other parents who have raised children who remain active in the Church. And I use suggestions from a small but convincing body of sociological studies on the faith lives of teens.

This book is for any parent interested in creating a faith-nurturing environment in his or her home. As I said, I'm one of the most unlikely Christian parents you could possibly imagine. I've made more mistakes than I care to admit. So if you're struggling with your faith and not sure what to do, I understand. If you've just come back to or into the Church and don't have a clue what to do with your children, I completely get that, too. If you're solid in your faith but want guidance in fostering an increasingly holy atmosphere in your home, welcome. My message to you is "You can do this."

Don't wait until it's too late. Now is the time. When your kids are grown, it will probably be too late for you to influence them. I know you're busy just trying to survive and keep the family going. Most likely you and your spouse are working, and quite possibly one of you is working extra hours to get ahead or just to make ends meet. But even with all that, don't neglect the spiritual aspects of your children's development. Everything I talk about here may seem like a lot to do . . . perhaps too much. Take it slow. You don't need to do all of it at once. Implement a few things, then when you're comfortable, add some more. But do something! Don't look back with regret on those childhood years and wish you'd worked on your own faith life, talked to your children more about God, and made a home where faith was nurtured and grown. *Now* is the time to prepare that ground and plant those seeds.

You can do this!

PART I
HOW DOES
FAITH WORK?

I was a Catholic who didn't believe in God. That is, until just before I turned thirty-three. They say faith is a gift. If that's the case, why do some people get it and others don't? Somehow, in my childhood, I was absent at that party.

Everything changed one Holy Saturday at a Navy base outside Tokyo, Japan. I was about to attend my first Easter Vigil, the most important liturgical celebration of the year for Catholics. Only two months earlier, I doubted there was a God, and now in a few short moments, I would celebrate his Resurrection from the dead. It was there I fully understood—for the first time—Christ was truly present in the Blessed Sacrament. I was startled and amazed to realize I had faith.

This book is an exploration of faith for Catholic parents—how to grow in faith and how to hand it on to your children. My quest to figure out what faith is and why mine was sidetracked, topics I explore in the next few chapters, became my mission to help Catholic parents discover the great beauty of the Catholic faith and teach them to effectively share that beauty with others—especially their own children. I want to help Catholic kids stop short of rejecting the Church the way I did. What I have learned through my quest is that religious education programs have holes and that parents are the key to filling them.

The truth is that kids need more than education to develop an active faith and personal adherence to God. Parish religious education programs and Catholic schools cannot match the faith formation potential of families. Fostering deep faith within a person requires intimate relationship, knowledge of that a person's deep needs, and a firm bond of trust. That's difficult to accomplish with ninety minutes once a week in a class of ten to fifteen (often more) students. As a parent, you have an intimate relationship with your children, know their deep needs, and have a firm bond of trust. Unlike parish catechists, you are in the perfect position to help your children develop deep faith. I know it seems daunting, but I think any parent can do this with a bit of study and some effort. You don't have to be a saint or a scholar to pull this off. The first step is to understand what faith is and how we get it. Without that knowledge, you're shooting in the dark.

1.
FAITH AT LAST

I was baptized into the Catholic Church as an infant. Like most Catholic kids I knew, I went to weekly religious education classes. They called it CCD (which, I learned years later, stands for *Confraternity of Christian Doctrine*). Southern Louisiana was Catholic country, and CCD was just what you did. For nine years, we all went, but it didn't mean a whole lot to us. We went to Mass on Sunday and CCD on Monday after school, and the rest of the week God never inhabited our thoughts. Along the way, we received the Sacraments of Penance (or Reconciliation, which many people refer to simply as *confession*), Eucharist (or First Communion), and Confirmation. I stopped attending CCD as soon as I was able—right after my Confirmation in eighth grade, though I continued attending Sunday Mass with my family.

By the time I started college at Louisiana State University (LSU), I was all done with the Church. There was no conscious decision to reject the Church; I just stopped going. I'm pretty sure I learned the basic tenants of Catholicism as a kid, but they held no spiritual meaning for me. The only thought I remember having about the Eucharist was that it tasted like cardboard.

FLYING AWAY FROM FAITH

While God wasn't on my mind in college, other things certainly were—such as girls and becoming a military pilot. I wanted to join the air force because my uncle was an air force officer. He taught math at the Air Force Academy in Colorado Springs, and spending time with him there gave me the flying bug. Air Force Reserve Officers' Training Corps (ROTC) at LSU led to full-blown infection, but after I saw Tom Cruise play a navy fighter pilot in the movie *Top Gun*, my interest switched to the navy. The romance of carrier flight ops, the allure of added danger, and the prospect of traveling the world was like a siren song that drew me in. The navy guaranteed me a slot in flight school if I could get through Aviation Officer Candidate School or AOCS (remember *An Officer and a Gentleman*?). So I quit college and signed up. Right before I left, I met a girl through a service organization affiliated with the Air Force ROTC. We dated long distance while I went through AOCS and then flight school in Pensacola, Florida. She pursued a master's degree in linguistics at LSU.

I finished flight school, got winged as a naval aviator, and a few months later married Shannon, the girl from LSU. My new bride had the exact same faith background as I did—she was a cradle Catholic who had left the Church in her teens for the same kinds of reasons. Like me, she felt no connection to the Church. We lived in San Diego for a few years and then transferred overseas to Atsugi Naval Air Facility in Japan. I had always wanted to live in Japan and was fascinated by the culture. Shannon's linguistics coursework focused on teaching English as a second language, so my posting was perfect for her. In Japan, through a series of events too long to record in full here, we returned to the Catholic Church.

COMING HOME AGAIN

Our coming back was a whirlwind. If you had been there and blinked, you might have missed it. We started seriously investigating Catholic teaching around Christmas 1997. By Lent, we were praying the Rosary every day and attending Mass regularly. Over the course of that Lent, we became more and more deeply immersed in the life of the Catholic community at the base chapel—working with a ministry to the homeless, going to daily Mass, and teaching religious education classes on Sundays. Yes, it's true: we could barely fog a spiritual mirror with supernatural life, but we were asked to teach fourth-grade CCD. I loved it. I wanted to share everything I was learning with anyone who would listen. I probably shared too much! Shannon was also asked to be a sponsor for a woman named Martha, who was preparing to become Catholic through the Rite of Christian Initiation of Adults (RCIA). She took that role very seriously; after all, she was learning, too.

So there I was, waiting to experience my first Easter Vigil, the high point of the liturgical year. It begins outside the church, after dark, with the priest's lighting a small bonfire, the new fire that represents the light of Christ, the light of faith, entering the world. Later, borne on candles in the hands of all who have gathered, this light illuminates the entire darkened church—it represents the faith of every individual believer overcoming the darkness of an unbelieving world.

Shannon, Martha, and I huddled together in the chilly evening air outside the base chapel. I wasn't sure what all was going to happen at the Vigil, but I knew Martha was going to receive her First Communion and I had done that. As we were about to go in, I turned to Martha and said, "When I was a kid before I made my First Communion, I always wondered what the bread tasted like." I continued with a chuckle, "Then I found out. It tastes awful—just like cardboard."

And at that moment it struck me: the host wasn't just bread . . . it was Jesus! I was joking about Jesus!

I was taken aback, shocked with what I had just said and the amazing reality of the Eucharist that was just beginning to sink in. Martha's face showed an uneasy look as well. I just smiled a little and shut up, embarrassed. We didn't say any more about that moment for the rest of the night. Though I had learned about the Real Presence as a child, before that night I had never believed in or cared what the Eucharist really was. It had never mattered that much to me. But that night, at that moment, it came to mean everything.

FAILED BY THE SYSTEM

That Easter Vigil experience changed my life. The Eucharist became more than an abstract concept to me; it became real and relevant. For the first time in my life, I had faith. I truly believed in this person, Jesus, who was real and alive and there. But more than that, I was overwhelmed by him. His truth penetrated everything I was. I wanted to follow his way of life, to think, judge, and act like him. I trusted he could lead me to happiness and fulfillment.

I began to study and seriously ponder the question of how I could have grown up in the Catholic Church not caring about God at all. It nagged at me. I had to know. Answering this question became a personal quest that eventually led me to leave my naval career and study theology at Franciscan University of Steubenville in Ohio. I wanted to know what faith was all about and what had gone wrong with mine.

In some important ways, my story reveals much of what's wrong with Catholic religious education today. I should have known faith. I should have believed in the Real Presence and had a personal relationship with God. My parents did all the "right" things and outwardly fulfilled the obligation they undertook at my Baptism to raise me in the Church. They took me to Mass each week, sent me through the Catholic religious education system, and saw to it that I received the sacraments. I was fully educated and officially initiated; after Confirmation I should have been on my way to becoming a practicing adult member of the Catholic Church.

But there was a slight hitch: I didn't want to be a member, and I didn't want to practice. The system had taught me everything except the *reason* why I should stay or care. The system didn't help develop my faith, and my parents didn't either. They trusted the system to do that and likely didn't know how to do more, which is the root of the problem for so many Catholic families today.

The average Catholic probably imagines that this system works like an assembly line. Go through the process and you come out on the other end fully equipped and ready to go, like a car with all the standard features. The notion that working through the process will set you on the path to heaven is widely accepted. And why wouldn't every parent believe in this process? It's the way most Catholic parishes are set up. However, it's not that simple. The standard features are not enough if the engine is missing. For the process to work, your children need more. Your children need *you*.

The sad truth is that my story is not uncommon. Youth and young adults are leaving the Catholic Church in droves. According to the Pew Research Center, four times more Catholics leave the Church than join. One out of every ten American adults is a former Catholic raised in the Church, and they most often leave before the age of twenty-three.[1] Those numbers are not just statistics. Every one represents a young person who reaches adulthood not knowing Jesus Christ in and through the Church. This saddens me because I believe the Catholic way is the best way to live. Those teens and young adults growing up without deep roots in Catholicism will instead find guidance, and identity, in the secular culture, their own desires for pleasure, and material success. That is destructive. We are failing to pass on to our children the attributes that truly matter: love for and faith in Jesus Christ, who leads us to the Father. With that faith comes a certain set of values and a moral code that lead us to eternal life with God in heaven. We are failing to help our children lead happy, fruitful Christian lives that will eventually help them reach heaven.

REFLECT

What was your religious life like growing up? Did you always have a strong faith or did you fall away? Where are you in your faith life today, and how has that affected your parenting style in regard to your children's religious education? Are you willing to work on deepening your faith to help your children?

PRAY

Find a quiet place where you can spend time alone talking to God. Tell him all your concerns regarding this project of handing on faith to your children. Relate to God your doubts, fears, and hopes for your family. If your faith life is not where you want it to be, ask him for insight into what you can do to strengthen it. Then take some time to listen for thoughts, intuitions, and inspirations. That's how God speaks to you.

LIVE

This book covers how to help your kids grow in faith, but you can—you actually *need to*—grow along with them. If you want your children to have a strong, mature faith, you must have one first. There's no way around this truth. Two sayings sum it up: "Faith is more caught than taught" and "You can't give what you don't have." They're overused and a bit cliché, but that's because they're true.

The first one is true in most areas involving behavior and character building, but it's especially true of faith. We look to pattern our lives after role models, people who are what we want to be in the future. Parents have the biggest influence over their children in this regard. Kids naturally pick up on cues about what is important in your life and adopt those things as important in their own lives.

The second saying complements the first. In many ways, faith is like an inheritance you pass down. What you say about faith has less impact on your kids if you're not living the faith. There's no credibility. Your kids may go along with you out of obedience, but your message won't be a part of them. And that's what it has to be. Don't worry; I'll help you build up your faith so your children can catch it from you.

2.
THE NECESSITY OF SAYING YES TO CHRIST

How could I be baptized and not have faith? The question plagued me. Faith is the foundation of the Christian life, yet what it is and how to develop it remain mysterious. Many parents mistakenly think that if they have their children baptized, enroll them in programs to *learn* about the faith, and have them receive the sacraments, their children will stay Catholic. But it often doesn't work that way. Faith doesn't automatically develop from reception of the sacraments and religious education . . . although those two things are important in nurturing faith.

So what is faith and how do you get it? It's the foundation of the Christian life, yet most don't understand the process of receiving and nurturing it. Catholicism is meant to be a life-changing, person-transforming conduit for grace. However, without faith, spiritual formation gets derailed. Catholicism becomes just another topic to be learned, a set of facts to be memorized and likely forgotten.

INVITED TO FAITH BY RICARDO MONTALBÁN

At thirty years old, I thought my life was complete. I was married to a beautiful woman, flew helicopters for the navy, lived in Japan, and traveled all over Southeast Asia. In flight school, I had wanted to fly F-14s, but hey, you can't have everything. I was living nine-tenths of the dream and loving it . . . except I wasn't. I was restless. I had spent my whole young adulthood moving toward this destination, but when I finally got there, I looked around and wondered, "Is this all there is?" I wanted more out of life but didn't know what. I had pursued a dream, but it wasn't spiritual; it was worldly, and in the end it wasn't enough.

So I started a spiritual quest to discover how to live with purpose. I studied Western philosophy, but that just gave me more questions. I studied Eastern philosophy and Zen Buddhism; they helped some but were too disengaged from human life. Finally, I settled on the New Age movement. Here was a step-by-step guide on how to live well and find your true purpose. Shannon was on a similar journey, so we studied together. Neither of us even considered the Catholic Church we had grown up in. What life-fulfilling spirituality was to be found in the Church? All it had was stupid rules made by old men in Rome who wanted to limit our lives and our freedom.

Shannon and I bought VHS tapes to learn about the New Age. That spiritual movement draws from a lot of different sources and mashes them together. Some of its sources are Christian, so ironically the New Age movement opened us to Christian concepts we had instantly rejected before. We watched tapes, read books, studied, and meditated. However, Shannon was soured on the whole business when we befriended a psychic healer from Australia who ended up scaring us half to death. After that experience, much to my surprise, Shannon began attending Catholic Mass again. What was even more surprising to me was that she liked it!

She encouraged me to join her, but I wasn't having any of it, so she did an end around: she ordered a tape about the apparitions at Fatima without telling me. I didn't want to watch it, but since we couldn't return it, I thought what the heck. That tape blew my world apart. In the apparitions, the Blessed Mother showed the children a vision of hell and said many people go there. The narrator was Ricardo Montalbán. (Some of you will know him as Khan Noonien Singh from the *Star Trek* universe or Mr. Roarke in the old television series *Fantasy Island*.) In his sophisticated accent, he issued a challenge that became an invitation to faith: "The children's testimony was truthful. Now, what are you going to do about it?" I was cut to the heart. I turned to Shannon and said, "If this is true, we're in big trouble. We're going to hell. We have to figure out if this is real!" That shocker began our journey back to the Catholic Church and to real faith in Jesus Christ.

BOTH DIVINE GIFT AND HUMAN COOPERATION

Infants receive the theological virtue of faith infused into their souls at Baptism. Theological virtues are like bridges between divine and human action; they configure souls for cooperation with the promptings of the Holy Spirit. Everything you believe about God and everything you do for him is the result of his action in your soul. Even the first inkling you have about believing in God is placed there by him. The theological virtue of faith gives you the supernatural *capacity* to believe—but that doesn't mean you *actually* believe.

The *Catechism of the Catholic Church* says faith is "both a gift of God and a human act by which the believer gives personal adherence to God . . . and freely assents to the whole truth that God has revealed."[1] The "gift of God" part is the theological virtue or the grace. The "human act" part is our cooperation with that gift. We receive the grace to believe; however, it is up to us to use that gift in the right way. We have to make the decision to believe. This part is indispensable.

Think of a seed. That seed contains a plant . . . in potential. It's not actually a plant yet, but given the right conditions it could be. If it's planted in good soil and watered, it will grow. With infant Baptism, faith is like the seed. It gets planted in the soul through God's gift of grace. There it awaits that human act, a decision to believe. Without the water of a person's free choice to believe, the seed of faith won't grow.

Faith is a response to the reality of God, a "personal adherence" and free assent. Moved by grace at the proper time, a person must make an *act of faith,* a voluntary commitment or pledge to be on Christ's side. The child baptized as an infant must be made aware of who Christ is and what he's done, how that child was created in love to share in the richness of God's glory, and how Jesus was sent to make that sharing possible through his Passion and death. This is the Good News or Gospel of Jesus Christ. The child must also be led to understand this great gift as a personal invitation to share in the Christian life and to know that a personal response to the invitation is required. Accepting the invitation leads to conversion, the decision to follow Christ and live in union with him.

ACTIVATING FAITH

Saying yes to Christ is not something we just come to naturally. Rather, this assent comes in response to explicit invitation from another who knows the joy of faith. We must be led to faith and accompanied in our discovery of God's calling to be his disciples. This invitation and personal accompaniment are what was missing in my faith life as a child. The teaching in my classes never touched me on a personal level, never really caused me to change my life in any way. I was never asked to make a real act of faith, and consequently I never consistently gave God my assent.

This lack of an evangelizing invitation to personal relationship with Christ persists in religious education programs today. The act of faith is the water that activates the seed. If a child is never led to a conscious decision to believe in God and follow him, to tend the soil of his heart, the seed of faith will likely stay dormant. The child is still baptized—that doesn't change. But the graces of Baptism aren't active. If nothing ever happens to awaken faith, this dormancy will continue into adulthood.

At the time I watched the video that startled me awake, several realities were converging. I was restless and desired more out of life, I was spiritually open and actively seeking, and I was primed by my New Age explorations to be more receptive to Christianity. My heart was at last fertile ground for the seed planted at my Baptism. That video delivered a powerful nudge for me to make a seed-activating act of faith. The message of the video—God is real, and there are eternal consequences to not believing that fact—shocked me out of my indifference to the Christian God and set me on the path to learning more. No one had ever challenged me to choose faith before. God wasn't real to me, and I didn't believe. Until that video, the choice to truly follow God had never been put before me in a way that reached me.

When I began to study Catholic teaching, I was blown away. It was everything I was looking for and wanted, supplying spiritual wisdom with a depth and richness I hadn't encountered anywhere else. I found that Catholic doctrine delves into the human condition and accounts for all its complexities and problems. It doesn't try to explain away human nature or seek to transcend it, but rather embraces it and lays out a plan for its fulfillment.

The more I learned, the more I realized I had never understood the full beauty of the Catholic faith. I kept saying to myself, "Why hasn't anyone ever told me this before? Why haven't I heard?" The fertile soil of my soul was watered. Faith was activated. I believed.

GOD'S CALL TO CATHOLIC PARENTS

So how could I be baptized and not have faith? The answer reveals the surprising truth about faith: Baptism is part of the equation, but it's not everything. Faith requires both divine and human contributions. God's grace is the first part of the equation; your decision to cooperate with that grace and to align yourself with him is the second. God is constant, so his gift of faith is always flowing to you. Unfortunately you are not constant, so you must make your decision over and over again throughout your life, or faith will fade and die.

The problem comes when those in charge of your children's faith formation (including you) fail to understand this dynamic, thinking that getting baptized, receiving the other sacraments, memorizing prayers, and being educated about Catholic teachings are enough to awaken faith. They are not. Abstract, theological knowledge rarely moves hearts toward conversion. People need more.

You can provide that "more." What happened to me and happens to thousands of Catholic children every year doesn't have to happen to your children. You are perfectly poised to make your children's souls fertile ground, prepare the soil, and activate their faith. This is your call as a Catholic parent, the mission entrusted to you at your children's Baptisms. It's a mission you're perfectly capable of accomplishing. You can do this.

REFLECT

Have you studied Catholic teaching as an adult? Or are you still operating from the theological understanding you developed as a teen or perhaps even younger?

Engaging the faith as an adult gives you a completely different perspective. You have different concerns and life experiences than when you were younger. You've done things you regret and seen things you'd like to forget. The Gospel message of Jesus will resonate more clearly with you. That's why it's tragic so many Catholics lose faith and interest in the Church as teens. They quit before Catholicism shines—not because the Church is different later but because they are. As with any relationship, your knowledge and understanding of God and your Catholic faith must grow as you grow.

PRAY

Find a quiet place where you can spend time alone talking to God. Ask him for strength and inspiration as you begin this important mission of nurturing your own and your children's faith. If you're not ready to begin or not sure you want to consider this task, ask for grace and guidance on his will for your children and your parenting. God can give you motivation that wasn't there before.

LIVE

Consider studying expertly presented Catholic teaching. Not what you get from the secular media, the History Channel, or people outside the Church who think they understand Catholicism, but well-credentialed Catholic theologians and pastoral leaders who know what the Church teaches. Great information can be found in books, videos, podcasts, or classes at your parish. I suggest beginning with Bishop Robert Barron's *Word on Fire* ministry. Bishop

Barron is a relevant, insightful thinker who engages our culture with well-reasoned Catholic thought. He will open your eyes to the depth and richness Catholicism brings to the world. You can listen to podcasts of his daily homilies, watch his videos on You Tube, or just read blog posts to start. He also has several excellent video series you can buy including his beautiful, ground-breaking work, the Catholicism series. The online hub for all these resources is wordonfire.org.

An excellent book that explains what Catholics believe and why is Scott Hahn's *Rome Sweet Home*. It was one of the first books I read in my journey back to the Church, and it's still a great resource. For twelve years, whenever I spoke with someone interested in joining the Church, more often than not this book influenced their decision. It's that good.

For a more in depth look at why we believe what we do, consider Frank Sheed's *Theology for Beginners*. Sheed provides a reasoned, comprehensive, yet concise theological explanation for the most common Catholic beliefs. If you crave the more intellectual approach, this one will not disappoint.

New Age gurus tout themselves as experts while spewing derision and misinformation about Catholic doctrine. I know because I've heard them and believed them, until I learned what the Church really taught from true Catholic teachers. I know for a fact there are many other Catholics out there who are being similarly misinformed. I'm betting when you hear how integrated and complete Catholicism really is, it will blow your mind. Take a look! It just might change your life!

3.
THE POWER OF
PERSONAL INFLUENCE

At this point, you may be feeling a bit daunted and wondering what you could do with your children that would be so different from what the parish is doing. Perhaps you feel you don't know the faith well enough to teach it. I'm guessing you don't have a degree in theology, or any theological training, and that's all right.

The goal in most parish programs is to give kids a systematic presentation of Catholic teaching. It's knowledge for the sake of knowledge. Intellectual formation. This is the wrong goal for young children. I don't want to downplay the importance of learning in depth what the Church teaches; that's an integral part of faith formation at the proper time. What you need to understand is that there's another, more important type of learning that needs to happen first, one that happens best within the family. It's the type of learning that awakens faith.

If theological knowledge is not the most important kind of knowledge, what is? After all, isn't religious education, well . . . you know, education? If the intellectual approach falls flat, what other kind of education is there?

CARDINAL NEWMAN
AND PERSONAL INFLUENCE

Someone who profoundly understood the answer to this question and acted on it was Blessed John Henry Newman. Newman was an Anglican priest and Oxford scholar who converted to Catholicism in 1845 at the age of forty-four. He became a Catholic priest and was eventually named a cardinal by Pope Leo XIII. Newman was an extremely effective teacher and evangelist. He attracted many loyal followers who were greatly moved by his preaching and personally attached to him. This was no accident. It was the natural result of his methodology for teaching the faith.

In a sermon written early in his Anglican career, Cardinal Newman asked how the ancient Church had been so successful in spreading Christianity throughout the world in a way that endured despite its many trials and difficulties. That's really our question, too. With all the obstacles to faith in our society, how can we pass on the faith to our children so that it lasts a lifetime?

After proposing many possibilities and shooting them all down, he concluded that the faith "has been upheld in the world not as a system, not by books, not by argument, nor by temporal power, but by the personal influence of such men as . . . are at once the teachers and patterns of it."[1]

Newman knew it wasn't just the excellence of the content that accounted for the enduring success of the Church. It was the way teachers passed on the faith to their students—through close relationships and personal examples of holiness—that made the faith endure.

Personal influence was a hallmark of Newman's thought. For him, this principle formed the very essence of the teaching and learning environment. "I say, then, that the personal influence of the teacher is able in some sort to dispense with an academical system, but that the system cannot in any sort dispense with personal influence. With influence there is life, without it there is none."[2]

GIVING THE SELF
ALONG WITH THE TRUTH

My professor at Franciscan University used to say that an effective catechist "never merely imparts knowledge. He gives himself with the truth adhering." Newman embodied this in the way he spoke and wrote. Newman didn't just give knowledge; he gave himself. Not many people teach the faith this way. Usually it's just about the facts. When on rare occasion you do find someone who teaches this way, hold on because it's powerful.

In addition to being penetrating, thorough, and insightful, Newman's teaching bore the power of personal witness. When he discussed a topic, he not only gave the doctrinal understanding of the subject, he also gave the background of how he came to understand it and why he believed it. Such authenticity is compelling in any type of persuasive speaking but doubly so when teaching religion. It lends credibility to what you're saying. Most students will accept a doctrine as true because the Church teaches it. However, they'll allow it to become part of their lives only if an instructor pulls back the curtain to expose personal convictions and motivations.

Newman was interested in the individual and in speaking to the heart. He aimed at getting what he called *real assent* from his listeners and readers. Real assent is an understanding and acceptance that comes from a concrete encounter with a topic; it involved perceiving a teaching personally and considering its effect on you as an individual, rather than its general or abstract effect. Newman believed that studying an idea from a purely intellectual view-point left the student distanced from the idea.

The opposite of real assent is *notional assent*—an assent based on universals and abstractions. Dr. John Crosby writes:

> Take the fact that I will one day die: I can assent to this either notionally or really. If notionally, then I assent above all to the fact that everyone dies, and I include myself in the universal mortality of human beings. But if I give a real assent to my death, then I experience myself not just as a logical part of "everyone" but almost as if I were the only human being; I experience my death as something supremely concerning to me personally. Then my assent shakes me to the roots of my being, raising my personal existence to an intense pitch, whereas the notional assent leaves me unmoved, almost as if I were just a spectator of my own future death.[3]

CONCRETE, EXPERIENTIAL, ENGAGED RELIGIOUS EDUCATION

This idea of being engaged with religion instead of merely a spectator on the sidelines is the key to what we're trying to achieve. So much of religious education today is notional. Catechists teach the faith from standardized textbooks created by publishing companies that cater to the masses. The presentation is purposefully average so it appeals to the broadest market. No book can fully recognize an individual child's dreams, desires, and difficulties. How could it? Teaching that comes solely from a textbook creates a merely notional assent, passive involvement, and a distanced and indifferent religion. Thus, students' lives are never touched by the real and personal. They remain unchanged by their religion because the religion they experience is bland, weak, and unspectacular.

Cardinal Newman's cure was to transform the notional into the real—to engage the spectator, bring him or her off the sidelines of intellectual passivity, and impart an awareness of the intersection between life and religious truth. For him, the crucial question is not *how is it true*, but *how is it true for you*? How does it affect your life, and what does it mean for your particular situation? That's the truth we need to bring out, and it can be done within the family. Family-based faith formation can solve the problem of merely notional religious education.

Human persons are moved to action not by intellectual abstractions but by personal influence and powerful example, as well as by engaging their imaginations with the concrete realities of life. When we interact with others personally, we open ourselves to deep encounter and change. Without that engagement and interaction, Catholicism is just a bunch of words and listless actions. To some, it will be logical, reasonable, even interesting, but will remain just one theory among many. Faith itself becomes notional—abstract and distant—rather than real.

As their mentor and guide in life, you're in the best position to help your children consider topics and issues personally, to take faith out of the abstract and make it concrete. Your openness to sharing your personal experiences and convictions provides the background that makes faith credible and attractive. That's why it's so essential for you to fulfill this God-given calling to participate in your children's faith development.

I'm not saying you have to do a full-blown religious education program in your home. You should still send your kids to the Catholic school or parish religious education program to get a systematic, intellectual education in the teachings of the Church, which require *notional* assent. But you will need to prepare the soil of your children's hearts and minds with *real* assent to the faith at home. If you are giving them a concrete, personal, real experience of religion at home, then religious education in the parish can be what it is and still work to your and their advantage. This is what I've done with my own kids, and it works. I guarantee you won't regret investing this time with your kids. They'll love it, too, and it will pay huge future benefits.

REFLECT

Are your attitudes toward religion and faith notional? Often we know the truths of the faith and perhaps acknowledge them as true, but that's as far as it goes. We don't really live by them. Does religious truth play a central part in your life? Does it shape your decisions? Or is it something you learned at one time and believe in but don't pay much attention to in your daily life?

Are you uncomfortable sharing your faith? Do you have trouble talking about your feelings regarding faith and how it clashes with your needs and desires? Do you think you would have trouble discussing this with your children?

PRAY

In your quiet time alone with God, reflect on your image of him and your relationship with him. If you've never thought of God as a person you could relate to, take a chance: ask him to reveal himself to you and give you an understanding of him as a person. Then spend some time listening. If you have a relationship with God already, ask him to deepen your awareness of him.

LIVE

If you've never engaged faith concretely or have only experienced Catholicism in a notional way, perhaps you should consider joining a faith-sharing group in your parish or getting a faith-mentor yourself. Many Catholics aren't comfortable talking about their faith. That's because we don't get much practice. We're mostly told to just believe . . . hence the problems! Like anything else, faith-sharing takes practice but is definitely worth the effort. This will open your faith to a whole new level. In the parish, I've seen people who never participated in faith-discussions, and didn't think they could, come alive from the experience. I would challenge you to give it a try. It will help you talk to your children and grow in your relationship with God.

4.
FOUR WAYS PARENTS ARE ESSENTIAL FOR HANDING ON FAITH

The example and personal influence of parents are indispensable for handing on faith to children. Official Church documents call the role of parents in the spiritual and moral formation of their children "primordial and inalienable" (*CCC*, 2221). The foundational influence of parents is so important that it's "almost impossible to provide an adequate substitute."[1] Parents are rightly the "first preachers of the faith"[2] and so essential that this educational role is "incapable of being entirely delegated to others or usurped by others."[3]

Parish religious education is meant to supplement and aid the faith formation happening in the home. However, this is frequently not the case. Most children receive religious education only from the parish. Why spend the extra effort? Because it's the most effective way.

From 2002 to 2005, Christian Smith and Melina Lundquist Denton, sociologists at the University of North Carolina at Chapel Hill, conducted a nationwide study, based on surveys and interviews, of teen religious involvement. They reported their findings in the book *Soul Searching: The Religious and Spiritual Lives of American*

Teenagers. I love this book because it interprets scientific research done at a secular university. Smith and Denton are sociologists who are not in ministry or affiliated with a Christian group, so their findings are based on data and have no Christian agenda. Nevertheless, their amazing insights back up my premise. Here are four ways, drawn from Smith and Denton's research, in which parents are essential for handing on faith to their children.

1. INFLUENCE

Parents matter . . . a lot! That's my biggest takeaway from *Soul Searching*. The finding actually surprised me. It's what I hoped for and wanted, but I wasn't completely sure the research would support my ideal. My fear was that MTV, Hollywood, and the merchants of cool on Madison Avenue have stolen the attention, money, and trust of American teens. Apparently, that's not the case. The research found that parents have a tremendous influence on the faith lives of their children, much more than their peers or other outsiders. Smith and Denton go so far as to call the influence parents exert over their kids "inescapable." Like it or not, you're always influencing your children. According to the researchers, it's not a question of *if* you are influencing them but of *what kind* of influence you are having on them.

This makes sense if you think about it. If you're a football fan and your kids grow up watching football with you every Sunday or going to games, they'll probably grow up loving football, too. Kids naturally pick up on what's important to parents and adopt the same interests. It's the family culture, and your example affects what your kids love and believe is important. I knew a guy whose family went to Disney World every year when he was growing up. Today he's a huge Mickey Mouse fan and takes his own family every year. Is that really so surprising?

The consequence of parents' having all this influence is that your example is vital. Smith and Denton argue that the single most important thing you can do to strengthen the faith lives of your children is to have a strong faith life yourself. "For in the end," they explain, parents "most likely will get from teens what they as adults themselves are. Like it or not, the message that adults inevitably communicate to youth is 'Become as I am, not (only) as I say.'"[4] Not many people like to hear this.

If you want your children to grow up to be good Catholics, be one yourself!

2. TEACHING THROUGH RELATIONSHIP

Part of the problem for parents is that teens often project an aloofness that's unnerving. Smith and Denton aptly call this "benign whateverism." Combine this detachment with the mysterious, insider nature of teen culture and the way media and movies exalt it, parents feel uncomfortable teaching teens religion and faith. They assume they're too "uncool" to reach them.

But the whateverism is a defense mechanism, and all too often adults fail to understand this. Smith and Denton suggest that parents and adults should not be shy about passing on religious beliefs to their children. They believe that the majority of teens are open to being taught by adults even if the kids don't realize it themselves or act interested. "Parents," they write, "need . . . to develop more confidence in teaching youth about their faith traditions and expecting meaningful responses from them."[5]

You don't see that kind of reticence in other areas of life. Parents have no problem sharing information about their favorite sports, music, or art. There's no reluctance to advise kids on school or careers; why not teach them about their religion? Probably because these other subjects are less personal. However, if you can extend your comfort zone past taking the family to Mass, you have the potential to profoundly reach your children.

Accepting teaching on beliefs and behaviors from another person requires a strong relationship and a deep level of trust. Ideally, no one could match the level of intimacy you have with your kids. Parents are perfectly poised to teach their children about life from a religious perspective and affect them in ways no one else can.

3. ARTICULATION, OR TALKING ABOUT FAITH

One pattern Smith and Denton noted from their interviews with hundreds of teens was the inability of teens to articulate their faith. The teens had no experience putting into words what they believed or thought about their faith. They were comfortable discussing their thoughts on drinking, doing drugs, avoiding STDs, and practicing safe sex, but on the topic of religion they didn't really know where they stood. This is likely because their parents talked with them about those other issues but never about their faith. Most parents have a vivid picture of what they want for their children, and it doesn't include drinking and driving, drug abuse, or premarital sex. Here the dangers are clear, and the consequences for poor choices tangible. Everyone knows it's a parent's duty to communicate these physical dangers to their kids. But are spiritual dangers as clearly defined? Do parents understand the consequences of loss of faith, and do they have those discussions with their kids?

I've observed that the more you talk about religion, the more you understand it. That may not necessarily be true for math, but it is for religion . . . and philosophy, too. In support of this insight, Smith and Denton mention philosopher Charles Taylor's suggestion that being able to communicate a concept or claim makes possible its being real for a person. Smith and Denton conclude, "So, for instance, religious faith, practice, and commitment can be no more than vaguely real when people cannot talk much about them."[6]

This echoes Cardinal Newman's analysis of real versus notional assent, covered in chapter 3: to really absorb religion, you can't remain benched on the sideline as a passive learner. For these truths to move from your head to your heart (where they need to be for faith to take root), you have to actively wrestle with them and engage them. Only then do they become real instead of merely vague or notional.

If you want your kids to develop real faith, you have to discuss your faith with them. Not just "don't do this because it's wrong" or "thou shalt not because the Church says so." I mean real discussions that honestly consider personal and cultural issues and problems, what the Church says about them, and how these teachings relate to life. In order to articulate faith, you have to internalize it and understand the reasons why you believe it. You have to own faith and make it a part of you. The only way to get there is through dialogue and figuring out why something is true for you.

4. RELIGIOUS PRACTICES

Smith and Denton discovered that activities or practices play a vital role in the faith lives of religiously active teens. "For the committed adolescent," they write, "religion is not simply a matter of general identity or affiliation or cognitive belief. Faith for these teenagers is also activated, practiced, and formed through specific religious and spiritual practices."[7] Smith and Denton saw the teens intentionally engaging in activities like going to worship services as a group, Bible reading, prayer, confession, ongoing faith formation, and service projects. These teens lived out their faith not simply by stoically surviving a long worship service once a week but by making their faith part of their everyday life.

I like the word *practice* for describing the things we do to live out our faith because that's exactly what we're doing—practicing. Activities in the Christian life should be thought of as practice for getting holy because they jump-start and increase faith.

If the concern is about kids' engagement in religious practices, why are parents essential? Because you are the initiator of good habits of religious practice, the keeper of the schedule, and the provider of transportation. When your kids are young, they won't get to Mass, read the Bible, pray, get to church for confession, go to religious education classes, or engage in service projects unless you make them and or take them. If you wait until they're old enough to do it on their own, they won't. You have to schedule time for these activities and build these habits into them. I address this in more detail in chapters 7 and 17, but right now I'll say that it helps if you do these activities with your children. Make them family activities, and you'll get a double bonus. You'll be an example to your kids, and it will do you a ton of good as well.

REFLECT

Does knowing how much influence you have on your children's faith bother you? Are you daunted by this information? Why? Is your faith life where you want it to be? Does considering that you might have to make a change put a damper on your enthusiasm for this project?

PRAY

Talk honestly with God about the questions above. How do they make you feel? Are you confident in your faith? Or are you afraid your example of faith doesn't measure up? Ask God for the grace to change and become more what your children need.

LIVE

Many Catholic parents aren't interested in being part of their children's faith formation. I understand. We're all busy, and what I'm talking about is not easy. It will take time and a lot of effort. You may not feel incredibly comfortable with the idea or up to the task.

But here's the thing: the current system of Catholic religious education is not working. We are not forming our children in faith. We are not teaching them to find God, so they are leaving. Half are going to Protestant churches and finding relationships with Jesus there. The other half are doing nothing, casting their lots with the culture and betting there is no God.[8] All Catholic parents need to hear and understand this message: You can make a difference. You can help your children know God and have his power working in their lives.

I've been on both sides of the coin, and I can tell you that there's no better way to live than in union with Jesus Christ and guided by the wisdom of the Catholic Church. Truly believing this, I'd be remiss as a parent if I didn't pass that worldview along to my children. I wouldn't be preparing them for life the best way I know. Make no mistake: by passing your faith on to your children, you are doing them a great favor.

Your children will pick up a moral and spiritual outlook from someone. Kids don't grow up in a vacuum. Someone will introduce your children to a worldview at some point, and it quite possibly could be significantly different from yours; maybe it will be unhealthy. The culture is all too happy to indoctrinate your kids. Personally, I want my kids to have my values and my understanding of the world. I've worked hard to come to that understanding and made a lot of mistakes in the process, mistakes I don't want my kids to make. I want them to have the best start at a fulfilled life.

So what do you say—will you take up the challenge? Are you in? The road may not be easy, but it will be rewarding. As one of my professors used to say, with God, life is never boring.

PART II
IS YOUR OWN
FAITH SECURE?

When I first started parish work, I met a man who ran a Catholic boy's club. It was like a youth group for kids younger than high school youth group age. He observed that every kid who joined the club fit into the categories Jesus talked about in the Parable of the Sower. Based on that, he could predict their success in the club, as well as in their spiritual lives. Further, he observed that the parent's influence almost always determined the category.

That man's experience fascinated me; it led me to consider the implications of this parable for parents and eventually to write this part of the book. Part I addresses how faith works, why the current institutional religious education system cannot on its own transmit faith, why parents are in a perfect position to fill the gap, and four pathways they have for handing on the faith to their children. I place great emphasis on parental influence in part I. In part II, I assert that your first step is to tend to your own faith. Why?

If you've ever been on an airplane, you'll get this right away. If a plane's cabin depressurizes during an in-flight emergency, everyone will pass out because the air is thin at high altitudes. There isn't enough oxygen. So if you're traveling with kids, the first thing you do is put oxygen masks on them so they won't pass out, right? That was my first thought, but it's completely wrong. Do that, and there won't be enough time to don your own mask.

You'll pass out and be unable take care of your kids, and they'll be too busy freaking out to get a mask on you. You have to secure oxygen for yourself first so you can help your children.

Faith parenting works the same way. You're traveling this faith journey together as a family. Your children are your responsibility, and no one will take care of them the way you will. You must secure your own faith first or at least continue to develop it while you're sharing it with your children; otherwise you'll all be passing out from lack of faith-oxygen. Your role is essential.

A PARABLE ABOUT SOIL, NOT SEEDS

The Parable of the Sower appears in all three synoptic gospels and is familiar to just about everyone. It's one of my favorites because Jesus actually explains it, but I'm often frustrated when I hear a homily or commentary on it because I think people miss the mark on its application to our lives.

In the parable, the seed is the faith-inspiring Word of God. That could be many different things—a homily, a class, or hearing the Bible itself. It could also be an inspiration from God or perhaps even an invitation from a friend leading you toward God.

The soil is your heart. Not the thing beating in the middle of your chest. Your spiritual heart. Theologically, it's the innermost part of you. It's the place where God speaks to you. It's where your thoughts, feelings, and decisions emerge from—the essence of who you are. It is where faith grows.

Usually the application of this parable centers on the action of the sower. He casts the seed far and wide, not caring where it lands. The meaning, some say, is that we shouldn't be selective about who hears the Gospel. We should tell everyone. Some receive it (those who have rich soil), others don't, and we should be okay with that. But I'm not.

I'm all for casting the seed. God is always extending his grace to us. But my concern is this: what do we do about those without perfect soil? Do we just leave them that way, unable to sustain faith? Does that mean they have no chance at salvation?

I look at the parable in a different way. When I hear the parable of the sower, I hear a story about soil, not seed. In the parable, the seed falls into four different kinds of soil. The condition of the soil mirrors the condition of our hearts, so the problems with the soil represent problems with our hearts.

In the parable of the sower, Jesus gives us a great gift in showing us the obstacles to receiving his Word and growing in faith. The good news is that Jesus never says you can't improve the soil. With his help, you can amend the soil of your heart, which is great because we all have these "heart" problems in greater or lesser degree. Your goal? Understand the soil of your heart and work at improving it.

5.
BREAK OPEN
THE HARD GROUND
OF YOUR HEART

And as he sowed, some seed fell on the
path, and the birds came and ate it up. . . .
These are the ones on the path where the
word is sown; when they hear, Satan immediately comes and takes away the word that
is sown in them.

—Mark 4:4, 15

The first time my father took me to the campus of Louisiana State University I was about eight years old. Having lived my whole life in Baton Rouge, where it is located, I knew LSU was a big deal. My father had been a student there twenty years earlier. We walked to the heart of the university, the Quadrangle or "Quad," a group of classroom buildings that form a rectangle (hence the name) with an open area in the middle. Most older universities have something like the Quad. It's usually the oldest part of the campus where the first classrooms were built. LSU's current site opened in 1925, so at the time of my first visit the Quad was almost fifty years old. The Quad buildings still surround a grassy area decorated with sprawling live oak trees today; at the time of that long-ago visit, the grass was also crisscrossed with dirt paths.

I asked my dad about the paths. Why were they there? He said they had formed over the years as students made their way to and from classes. I imagined it had probably been just a grassy field at first. But as the logical routes got trampled, more students walked them and eventually there was less grass on them. Over the years, thousands of footsteps compacted the earth so that nothing could grow there. The ground was just too hard and exposed. By the time I became a student there a decade later, those same dirt paths had been covered over with concrete. Cement secured their place. And why not? Nothing would ever grow on them.

The first type of soil encountered in the parable is the soil on the path. When the seed falls there, it lies out in the open for the birds to eat. The seed cannot penetrate the path because its soil is too hard and packed down from years of use. Your heart can be hard, too; you can shut God out, turn your face from him, so that his Word can't penetrate or take root in your heart and nothing of God can grow there.

HOW YOUR HEART BECOMES HARD

Why do we harden our hearts against God? Sometimes it's fear. Being afraid of the unknown can lead us to act contrary to God's revealed truth. Following God can sometimes put us on the margin of our comfort zones. It's much easier and safer to keep to your own plans and agendas. Sometimes we decide that following God isn't feasible or just plain won't work, so we don't listen. Sometimes we doubt that God will give us everything we need, so we block him out. Also, there are times we just downright want things contrary to what God says is good for us. Our desires go against God's will, so we shut him out. Harden your heart to God long enough and it will become too hard-packed to let him in again. At least until something comes along to break up that hard ground.

Hardness of heart keeps us from understanding God's plan and the joy that comes from following him. In Matthew's gospel, Jesus likens the seed on the path to "when anyone hears the word of the kingdom and does not understand it" (Mt 13:19). St. Paul says that people who are outside of Christ are "darkened in their understanding . . . because of their ignorance and hardness of heart" (Eph 4:18). When your heart is hardened against God, even miracles don't mean anything to you. Jesus fed five thousand people from five barley loaves and two fish, and yet the same people who ate that day still asked for proof of who he was. Of course, lack of understanding just contributes to greater hardness of heart. It's a feedback loop.

VULNERABILITY TO ATTACK

The parable teaches that doubt and fear also come from the outside—from the enemy, Satan. Remember, Jesus explains that the birds that eat the exposed seed are Satan snatching away God's Word from your heart. The Holy Spirit gives peace, assurance, patience, and joy, but only if you let him in. If God's grace is not active in your heart, you're vulnerable to spiritual attack. It's not pleasant to think about, but it's most certainly real.

Alone, you're no match for the doubt and fear that Satan throws at you. You just aren't. Try to fight him on your own and you'll lose every time. Doubt snatches away peace. Fear destroys faith.

It's the first struggle, the fundamental question of relationship with the Divine since Adam and Eve—does God really love me? Can I trust him to take care of me? The solution is simple but not easy. The thing you have to do is the thing you find most hard—commit yourself to God's loving care and allow him to lead you. Trust breaks open the hard-packed heart.

Old Testament Israel in Exodus is the quintessential example of hard-heartedness in the Bible. God sent the ten plagues, parted the Red Sea, and rescued them from slavery by destroying Pharaoh's army, but still the Israelites doubted God and wanted to follow their own path. At one point when they had nothing to drink, they accused Moses and God of plotting to kill them. They were so convinced of this that they wanted to turn around and return to slavery in Egypt. Instead of raging against God, all they had to do was trust and ask for help. That's what Moses did. He asked in faith and got those hard-hearted whiners everything they needed. The problem? It wasn't always what they wanted (see Ex 17:1–7, 20:2–9).

DARING TO TRUST IN GOD

It's been said that if you can't find your own sins in the sins of Israel, you're not looking hard enough. Their struggle is everyone's struggle. We all have trouble trusting God and following where he leads. We want to be in control. As I look back over my life with God, it's easy to see that Israel's struggle is my struggle, too. I recognize the great gifts God has given me, and I know in my heart that he's on my side, yet still I question him every step of the way. I doubt. I worry. But always I cleave to him and do my best to trust that his way is the best way.

Trust comes from prayer, ideally meditative prayer in which you reflect on God's Word in the Bible, take time to listen, and talk to him. God wants to lead you as he led Israel in the desert. He wants to break through that hard-packed heart and give you his peace. But if you're always struggling against him, not letting him hold you like the child that you are, he can't give you what you need. Also, if you're not taking time to listen to and understand him, you'll never see the path to happiness he has laid out for you. In the end, where God leads me is usually better than what I dream up for myself. God's plan for you is good. Trust him.

REFLECT

How willing are you to adopt the way of life God says will lead to true happiness? How willing are you to give up what you know to follow God? You have hopes, dreams, and desires. In your experience, have your plans led to real happiness or to frustration? More to the point, what do you want for your children? Do you want them to navigate life on their own following society's often-destructive worldview or guided by the life-giving wisdom of God?

PRAY

Take some time in prayer to thank God for his love and mercy. Tell him you know he wants the best for you even though at times you get scared and doubt. Tell him you're sorry for shutting him out and stubbornly doing things your own way, even at times becoming hostile to his voice and his grace working in you. Ask for help in trusting him and living according to his truth. Ask him to break up the hard-packed earth of your heart and allow his Word to take root within you. Then listen for his response.

LIVE

Children's lives are built on trust. They trust you to provide for them, to keep them safe, warm, fed, and alive. Is that trust misplaced? I certainly hope not! If you know how to give good gifts to your children, how much more will the Father give to you (see Mt 7:11)? The answer is a lot more!

Your children trust you. They will learn to trust God from following your example and seeing the good gifts that flow from God to you. By observing your attitude of trust, your children will develop that attitude as well—but you must communicate it. Let them know how you trust in God. Pray daily as a family for the things you need. Pray with them privately about the things they need. Most important, share your victories. Let your children know how God is moving in your life and answering prayer. Show them where he's blessing you and your family. This is powerful.

Here are a few resources for learning about prayer that grows your trust in God. Jim Beckman's *God Help Me: How to Grow in Prayer* contains an excellent structure for conversational prayer he calls the "Essential Dynamics of Prayer." *Prayer Primer*, by Fr. Thomas Dubay, lays out the fundamentals of Catholic spirituality and presents a comprehensive chapter on a classic method of Christian meditation. Finally, two works by Fr. Jacques Philippe, *Searching for and Maintaining Peace* and *Time for God*, explain the principal aspects of placing your whole trust in God and how to pray with that goal in mind—both indispensable for practicing a fruitful and authentic Catholic spirituality.

6.
DEEPEN YOUR ROOTS

Other seed fell on rocky ground, where it did
not have much soil, and it sprang up quickly,
since it had no depth of soil. And when the
sun rose, it was scorched; and since it had
no root, it withered away. . . . And these are
the ones sown on rocky ground: when they
hear the word, they immediately receive it
with joy. But they have no root, and endure
for a while; then, when trouble or persecu-
tion arises on account of the word, immediately they fall away.

—Mark 4:5–6, 16–17

Faith is a tenuous, often fragile thing. In the parable, the second
batch of seed falls on a rocky place where the soil is shallow. It's
rich enough for the plants to quickly grow, but it's not deep. Plants
that grow there can't dig roots deep enough to find water, so when
conditions are harsh they quickly wither and die.

We can create "shallow soil" conditions in our hearts as well by
failing to understand the demands of Christian life. Being Christian doesn't eliminate hardship. The message of God's love, ten-
derness, and fatherly care is attractive, but often people don't get
the full picture. They don't form deep faith roots, so when harsh
conditions come, their faith withers and they fall away.

Trials will come. It's a fact: our infinitely perfect and totally loving God permits trials. For many, this seems counterintuitive. If God is completely in control, why would he allow suffering? Doesn't he want us to be happy? Yes, God does want us to be happy, but more than that God wants us to be holy. The path to holiness sometimes involves hardship.

WHY TRIALS?

I learned something about the purpose of trials at Aviation Officer Candidate School (AOCS), a fourteen-week officer boot camp for navy pilots. Each class had a marine corps drill instructor, and ours was Gunnery Sergeant Massey. He was a small man with a voice like thunder and a penetrating stare that could cut you in two. When he spoke/yelled, he wove a tapestry of curse words that could almost be classified as art. He destroyed us, then re-worked us, and in the end, we learned to trust him completely.

During the first week, which ironically was the hardest part of the whole program, a senior candidate told us that drill instructors didn't act randomly. They did everything for a reason. "Gunnery Sergeant Massey knows the program," he said. That meant all the harsh words, ridiculous commands, and encouraging words were calculated for a certain effect. The fourteen weeks were planned out to make us the combat pilots we wanted and needed to be. "Gunny knows the program" became our mantra when we got our butts kicked particularly hard or just needed to remind ourselves why we were there. And honestly, when we looked back on our experience after completing flight training and donning our "Wings of Gold," we knew that senior candidate had been right. Massey had drilled things into us that seemed useless at the time, but later proved to be valuable skills.

Sometimes, when life is hard and I'm feeling discouraged, I think about my experience at AOCS. I realize that God is like a drill instructor—the perfect drill instructor. Everything he does is planned out to make me the saint I want and need to be. I have to trust completely that God "knows the program" and that whatever happens in my life is happening for that ultimate reason.

St. Ignatius of Loyola was a soldier, a priest, and eventually the founder of the Society of Jesus, a religious order known today as the Jesuits. He came up with nearly the same explanation I just gave for understanding the purpose of trials in life, only much better because he's a saint. Here are three reasons, adapted from the teachings of St. Ignatius, why God permits trials in our lives and what graces we can receive from those trials:

1. Sometimes trials do come because you're off track and God is trying to bring you back. People think hardships such as family conflict, getting fired, or receiving a DUI are God's punishment. But trials like these can be a mercy. God's ultimate goal is for you to be with him in heaven. Whatever gets in the way of that goal is evil. Whatever contributes to it is good. From this viewpoint, punishment from God would be to leave you alone and let you continue in your sin. Trials might simply signal that something in your life needs to change. A shock can alter your perspective so that God's message to transform your life comes through loud and clear. The grace God wants you to receive in this instance is *conversion*.

2. Another reason God allows trials is to strengthen your resolve when times get tough. The grace here is *spiritual learning*. God already knows your character; he doesn't have to test you to figure that out. But *you* don't really know your character until you're tested. Trials give you an opportunity to resist what might be destructive in your life and so come to know your

spiritual strength; they help you know God better and so grow closer to him.

3. Finally, trials bring the realization that you need God. The truth is we can do nothing without him. Unfortunately, we often think we can do everything without him. When God allows you to get into a tight spot, you concretely realize the truth of the former statement and the lie of the latter: you can do many things, but you need God's help to do them. God wants to help you. All you have to do is ask. Through hardship, God wishes you to receive the grace of *humility*, the virtue that allows a true estimation of your strengths, your weaknesses, and your profound need for him.

HOW TO GROW DEEP FAITH ROOTS

Your mental attitude during trials determines how well you handle them. Here are some approaches that strengthen resolve and increase faith instead of leaving you sad, confused, and broken.

First, always try to see God's hand in the trial. He will give you the strength to endure and overcome. Consider which of St. Ignatius's categories the trial fits into. This helps you discern the grace of the trial and what you can learn from it. If you can find meaning in your suffering, it takes on a different character; frankly, that is the beauty and power of Catholicism. Difficult circumstances that seem meaningless can still have purpose and hope.

Second, stay active. Don't just passively sit back and allow a trial to consume you. If you hide yourself away in your own private pity party and never take action, you'll be overwhelmed. Instead, beg God in prayer to take away the trial or give you the strength to endure it. Meditate on the good things God has done for you in the past and read/study Bible passages that reveal the Father's merciful love. Lastly, engage in some spiritual exercise, devotion, or penance that will draw you closer to God. This counters the heaviness and lack of trust that closely follow unfavorable life situations.

So then, you've weathered the trial and things are going great again; now you can just put your feet up and enjoy the good life, right? Wrong! You keep up all your spiritual practices—prayer, meditation, and examination of your life and habits. In good times, these devotions, practices, and penances become your ongoing preparation for the next struggle. St. Ignatius made one thing perfectly clear: trials will come. Just expect them. So don't get lazy when everything is going your way. Build into yourself the habits and behaviors that can weather the harsh conditions with a sense of meaning, purpose, and peace.

This is how you create the conditions for deep roots in your faith. You cultivate an expansive, fatherly vision of God. You learn to discern the grace in tough situations and develop an arsenal of spiritual tools to deal with the hard times. Real faith and relationship with God are like a family bond. Ideally, family members never give up on each other. They never stop loving even when they don't get along. When things get rough, that's when the love kicks in. When things aren't perfect, that's when the commitment really shows.

REFLECT

Who is God to you? Is he your pawn, your puppet, your genie in a bottle who gives you the good things you want when you want them? Or is he a loving father who gives you what you need when you need it to help you grow as a person? A genie is under your control and follows your agenda. He brings out the age-old temptation to bend God's power to your will. A father is not under your control. He guides you because you don't yet know the way. In the end, which is more helpful?

The Bible says we shouldn't lose hope when God gives us hard lessons. "Endure trials for the sake of discipline. God is treating you as children; for what child is there whom a parent does not discipline?" (Heb 12:7). Only if he didn't care about you would he leave you without discipline. God wants you to grow in spiritual maturity and holiness. Sometimes that requires tough love. We have to trust that he knows what is best.

PRAY

How do you feel about God's allowing hardships and trials? Does it test your faith? Do you wonder about why there's evil in the world? Do you think God should do more about it? Talk openly to God about this. If you're angry about it, tell him. Don't keep it inside. God is big: he can handle it. Let him know what you're struggling with, and then listen to what comes back in the quiet of your heart.

LIVE

Once you deepen your own faith roots, you have to create the conditions for deep roots in your children's faith lives. Understanding the truth of what Christian life really is will be a tremendous gift to them. Tragedy will strike. They will be disappointed. They won't get everything they want, and their hearts will be broken. Help them understand this in the context of God's fatherly love, and give them the spiritual tools to deal with life's trials.

7.
CLEAR AWAY YOUR THORNS

Other seed fell among thorns, and the thorns grew up and choked it, and it yielded no grain. . . . And others are those sown among the thorns; these are the ones who hear the word, but the cares of the world, and the lure of wealth, and the desire for other things come in and choke the word, and it yields nothing.

—Mark 4:7, 18–19

Have you ever noticed that the plants you treasure are hard to grow, but the ones you hate are impossible to keep away? When I bought a house, I started gardening. I was amazed at how easily weeds grow. If you're not careful, you'll have more weeds growing in your beautifully planned garden than you have flowers. Those interlopers just take over!

There are weeds in the human heart as well. They are the things of the world that draw your attention away from God. You can plant the beautiful truths of God in your heart, but if you're not careful, weeds can easily grow and choke them out. For most people, just about anything is more interesting than religion and God.

In fact, the majority find any talk of it and him downright boring. It's definitely not difficult to find distractions.

We all have a tendency to put God on the back burner and relegate him to unimportance. It's a consequence of the Fall. God doesn't innately occupy the most important place in our lives. I find it disturbingly easy to go about my daily business without acknowledging him or praying to him, and I work for the Church! It takes conscious effort to put God at the forefront of your thoughts and give him the number one spot he deserves, but that's what you're called to do.

The problem in this scenario is not that the soil is poor but that it isn't being tended. The plot needs weeding. If you want God's Word to grow your heart, you have to give it room. You have to weed out those things that most distract you and keep you away from progress with God. In the parable, Jesus speaks of three categories of weeds (what he calls thorns) that can crowd out the spiritual life: worldly cares, the desire for money, and the desire for other things. Let's look at these one by one and see what we can do to remove them.

WEEDING OUT WORLDLY CARES

The first kind of thorn is worldly cares. What are they? Think about everything that goes into making a living and maintaining a home. You spend all day with the worries and pressures of your job. Then you come home to cooking, cleaning, laundry, and paying bills. You also have to take care of your kids, your spouse, your dog . . . It never ends. When do you have time for God? He can wait, right? There are way more urgent things that need attention now. That attitude slowly and progressively crowds God out of your life until he's gone.

The urgent is the enemy of the important. It's all too easy to let the urgent take over your life, but God and family should take precedence over work. In my heart I know that, but there are always so many things that need to be done. There's always one more task at work, one more thing to write before I forget, or one more job around the house that needs to be done. I tell myself there's plenty of time to connect with God; he'll understand if I skip prayer just this once, right? But once turns into twice and then three times—then before I know it, I haven't prayed all week. I rationalize that my kids will understand if I don't hang out, but soon that turns into never spending time with them.

There are always urgent priorities that demand your attention. The only way to make sure you don't neglect what's important is to make it official: you have to schedule it. Fill in an actual "appointment with God" on your calendar. I know it seems strange to calendar your prayer—kind of like scheduling a shower—but if you leave your prayer time to chance, the urgent will always win out. Trust me on this one; I'm the king. The same thing goes for other extremely important but seemingly less urgent things like family time. You only have so much time before your kids are grown and beyond your influence. Don't neglect to prayerfully prioritize the important so the urgent doesn't rob you of the greatest things in life.

WEEDING OUT THE LURE OF WEALTH

The next sort of thorn in the parable is wealth or riches. There's no shortage of warnings about money in the Bible. Jesus pretty much trashes it in the gospels. Would it ever be possible for a camel to pass through the eye of a needle (see Mt 19:24, Mk 10:25, and Lk 18:25)? Attachment to money can be spiritually dangerous.

Money is so tempting because it can falsely promise security. It's easy to believe that if you have enough money, you are protected against hardship that might result from unexpected problems. Then it becomes easy to turn away from God thinking you don't need him. Of course, that's not the case. Tragedy is indifferent to bank accounts.

On a deeper level, there's the pervasive attitude that the things you buy with money can bring you happiness. We all know in our hearts that isn't true, but it certainly feels true sometimes, doesn't it?

Happiness can never come from having material things. Possessions are dependent and vulnerable. When the luster of "new" fades, the only remedy is to acquire another new thing. To keep that thing-fueled happiness high, you need constant fixes of "new." Money and material things don't satisfy because you can only possess what is less than you, and what is less than you can never fill your heart. For your heart to be filled, you must be possessed by what is greater, and that's God.

The key to taking money out of the center is to give it away in planned giving or a *tithe*. The ideal tithe is 10 percent of your gross pay. It should go to your parish and other charities. Tithing is not easy when you first start, so you might have to work your way up to that amount. Start with 5 percent or even 1 percent if that's what you can manage. As you get more comfortable, increase the amount. Set up an automatic withdrawal from your bank account so you don't have to think about the money leaving (and aren't tempted to keep it sometimes). We've done a 10 percent tithe for many years, and it has brought us great blessings. Once you get tithing into your mindset and your budget, believe me, you'll see the blessings, too.

WEEDING OUT THE DESIRE FOR "OTHER THINGS"

The last thorn is the desire for "other things." That's pretty vague. Luke 8:14 clarifies a bit with the phrase "pleasures of life." This is indeed a sticky thorn because life is indeed pleasurable. Does weeding out the pleasures of life mean God doesn't want you to enjoy life?

When I first came back to the faith, I was confused by an apparent contradiction. It seemed like the saints who spoke the most about joy didn't enjoy themselves much. St. Francis of Assisi was known as the Troubadour of God's Love, the giddy herald of the Great King happily announcing the Gospel of Christ. However, he fasted continually and practiced the most austere penances. He never ate anything but stale bread or allowed himself any material pleasures. How was that enjoying life? It just seemed miserable, like he despised life and wanted to torture himself.

St. Francis was an extreme example of how to undermine the dangers of this thorn. He understood our hearts are drawn like magnets to the many wonderful things in life. We form attachments to beautiful things, pleasurable things. Sometimes those things are good and don't present a problem. Sometimes they're good but our attachments present distractions to union with God. Other times we get attached to things that are not at all good and those attachments lead us to distance ourselves from God.

You must weed your heart of attachments to things that are intrinsically evil and destroy God's life in your soul. They grow a lot easier than you think and they're hard to give up! But you develop the strength to do that by voluntarily denying yourself things that are good from time to time, such as eating good food (fasting), avoiding meat on Fridays (abstaining), or giving away money you could use to buy something fun (almsgiving). This will strengthen your ability to say no to sin and yes to God. Eventually you build up the ability to weed out things you're attracted to, but prove to be a distraction. It guarantees you stay well clear of things that are evil.

Despite what it looked like, Francis didn't hate the world or his humanity; he loved them. But he loved them in God, not in themselves. If you love created things in God, and your soul more than created things, then denying yourself pleasurable things for the good of your soul, and God, is a good decision. Francis took this to the limit. Ironically, he ended up loving the things of the world more because he loved them like God, without fear or selfish desire.

REFLECT

The key to all three thorny-soil situations is the same: God must be at the center of your life. If he isn't, life just doesn't work. We have a tendency to place our latest passion, desire, or problem at the center of our lives and allow all our other pursuits to revolve around that center. We fit God neatly into place on that carousel as well, exactly where we want him. And everything is fine . . . for a while.

But God can't be compartmentalized or arranged in a neat little section of your life. He's bigger than that. He's expansive, all-encompassing, transcendent. You don't fit him into your life: you fit your life into him. When God isn't at the center, life gets off-kilter—it continues to spin, but it wobbles and eventually breaks. When God is at the center, everything else is balanced and falls neatly into place.

What gets the most time in your schedule? What do you spend the most money on? The things that get your time and money are likely the most important in your life, the things that occupy the center. What would it take for you to put God at the center? What would you have to give up? How might that help you with relationships, finances, and peace of mind?

PRAY

In your prayer today, be honest with God about your weakness. Talk to him about all the thorns in your heart and how they take up so much of your attention. Then spend some time listening to what he says to you. Ask God to be the divine gardener of your heart. Ask him to weed your heart of all the distractions that keep you from living for him completely. Ask for help in giving him pride of place at the center of your heart.

LIVE

Out of all the thorns, probably the most dangerous are the never-ending lists of activities and interests that capture our hearts. Religion is just one player in the tightly contested battle for time, attention, and energy. Usually religion loses. By far the biggest offender is sports. Let's be honest, though; the responsibility for these thorns doesn't rest with kids. Parents are the ones prioritizing sports and other activities over Mass, religious education, and devotional practices. I'm not saying kids shouldn't be active, but time is a precious commodity. You have to weed your children's schedules to allow space for God.

Your children will naturally look for happiness in possessions just the way you do. You'll have to set the tone. I think it's important to limit them here. Even if it's within your means to give them everything they want and more, don't. It's okay for them to deal with wanting; that's life! Teach your children to curb product lust when they're young. It will only get worse. Children should also tithe on their allowance and gifts right from the start. Condition them to expect that 10 percent of what they get goes back to God.

Put a positive spin on it—tell them they get to keep 90 percent and only have to give back 10 percent to God. That's great, right?

I'd like to say a few words about video games. I don't think they're bad. They're fun. Too fun. If ever there was a potential thorn, this is it. They can be like a drug. Once you get started, it's difficult to stop. And after you stop, it consumes your thoughts and draws you back. Play too much and it's all you can think about, and all you want to do. Kids will neglect school work, household duties, and physical activity to maintain their video game habit. You should limit your children's video game time to establish a balance in your child's life.

While most video games aren't harmful in themselves, that doesn't apply to all. I see parents allowing kids to play adult (M-Rated) games with adult content. Many of my kid's friends play the Grand Theft Auto series where players can enter strip clubs, get lap dances, watch someone having sex (animated sex, of course), or pick up a prostitute and shoot her in the face. People record their sessions and post them on You Tube, so you can watch them yourself if you don't believe me.

Perhaps parents aren't aware of what's actually in the game. I don't know. I do know letting your child interact with those kinds of images in such an immersive environment is extremely dangerous. You're allowing the most toxic thorns possible into the garden of your child's heart. It will scar them. At the least, please consider playing M-rated games with your children to monitor what they're seeing and experiencing.

8.
TILL YOUR FERTILE GROUND

> Other seed fell into good soil and brought forth grain, growing up and increasing and yielding thirty and sixty and a hundredfold. . . . And these are the ones sown on the good soil: they hear the word and accept it and bear fruit, thirty and sixty and a hundredfold.
>
> —Mark 4:8, 20

So you've removed all the obstacles to grace: you've softened your heart, deepened your faith roots, and weeded out all the distractions and temptations. You've finally arrived. The seed of faith can grow and thrive in your heart. But wait, there's more work to be done—that's how it always is with something really worth doing. Did you notice that even though all the soil in this last scenario is good, some patches produce a better yield than others? If it's all good soil, why doesn't it all have the same yield? Clearly some patches of soil must be more fertile than others.

I want my faith to yield a hundredfold, not thirtyfold. How about you? Well, now the real work begins—the work of fertilizing that soil, of feeding your heart with spiritual nutrients. After all,

God is infinite. There's always further you can go, and believe me, you want to go further. That's where you find gold.

After getting shocked awake by the Fatima video, I set about investigating Catholicism. I needed to find out if it was true. In the context of the last few chapters, I guess you could say my hardened heart was dynamited open, and I was willing to learn. One thing Shannon and I did right during our time of investigation was remaining open. Every time we came across a new suggestion for a devotion or religious practice, we jumped in. That inspiration was a great grace from God. We could easily have dismissed all those practices as too much trouble . . . but we didn't. We figured diving in was the only way to find out if Catholicism was real.

Here are some practices we found that can help you grow in holiness after you've opened yourself to God.

THE ROSARY

At Fatima, the Blessed Mother asked the faithful to pray the Rosary every day. Since the Fatima apparition was the big motivation for our new journey, the Rosary was the first devotion we undertook. However, we didn't have a clue how to pray it. I had seen it done at funerals and once or twice at my great-aunt's house, but I didn't know how to do it on my own. Shannon didn't either. So we got a book that walked us through step-by-step—literally!—starting with the basics of what prayer goes with what bead and introducing us to all the mysteries. We started praying the Rosary every night.

Meditation guides that elaborate on the mysteries are the key to regular Rosary prayer. Without them, the Rosary can quickly become tedious. The real power of the Rosary lies in meditating on the mysteries. These vignettes from Jesus' life present the pivotal aspects of our salvation. Continued reflection on them will transform you. Guide books help you mine the riches of these stories.

Some books we used presented scriptural Rosaries that told the story of each mystery with Bible verses in between each prayer; others were lengthy meditation books where we read a paragraph or two of explanation about the mystery before we said the prayers. When we burned out on one, we'd start another. I suggest picking up an assortment of these meditation guides. They will skyrocket your knowledge of the Faith and help you gain so much more from the Rosary.

SUNDAY MASS

Then Shannon read that it was essential to go to Mass on Sundays. It's funny to say now, but we didn't know it made a difference what day of the week we attended. We were going to a Wednesday night Mass dedicated to Our Lady of Perpetual Help, one of Mary's many titles, but we weren't regularly going on Sundays. We started.

If you're not going to Mass regularly on Sundays, it's essential that you start. Sunday is the primary day of worship. It's the time the Lord has set aside for us to put away the distractions of life and focus on him. You receive immense graces and spiritual benefits from Sunday Mass. You may find it tedious and difficult to get through with kids, but the rewards are incredible.

To get more out of the Mass, read the Bible readings and spend some time thinking about them ahead of time. You can find them online at the United States Conference of Catholic Bishops' website (usccb.org). You can also go to the St. Paul Center for Biblical Theology (stpaulcenter.com) for solid commentary on the Sunday readings that situates them within the context of the whole Bible and the story of salvation. It will open your eyes to the beauty and integration of God's revelation in Scripture. I explain more about this in part III. You can also choose from among a multitude of devotionals for delving into the Sunday Mass readings with children.

EUCHARISTIC ADORATION

Another time Shannon dug up something on the Internet about adoration. Apparently—and I didn't know this—you could go spend time with Jesus present in the Blessed Sacrament and that would be good for your spiritual life. Go figure! Shannon said we should be doing this, too . . . so we did. It brought an incredible boost to our spiritual lives.

I cannot emphasize enough the importance of Eucharistic adoration. There is nothing else like it for growth in faith and in the spiritual life. I'll admit, it takes some getting used to, and it is not easy at first. A lot of people drift off, but hey, even St. Thérèse of Lisieux fell asleep in adoration, so snoozing with Jesus can't be terribly wrong. If you put your time in, God will reward you. He will flood your heart with his peace and make you never want to leave.

It may seem mundane to sit in a room with the Eucharist, but it's amazingly effective. I liken it to sunbathing, soaking in the rays of the sun until your skin slowly transforms from pasty pale to a golden glow. Eucharistic adoration is "Son-bathing," soaking up the grace of the Son, Jesus Christ, which is radiating from his presence in the host. After a while, your soul will get a toasty, golden glow. And the best part? You can stay as long as you want and you won't get burned . . . physically or spiritually.

THEOLOGICAL STUDY

We continued studying. Actually, we studied voraciously. As in the past, we got tape sets and videos, but now instead of listening to the New Age gurus, we gobbled up Catholic conversion stories, theology talks, and Bible studies. The chaplain's office at the army camp a few miles away had an entire set of videotapes on salvation history by Scott Hahn. I eagerly plowed through the entire fifteen-part set.

I consider continuing study to be one of the essential elements in my long-term conversion. The doctrine of the Church is rich and beautiful but also somewhat complex and hard to grasp. Some of the most controversial topics are the ones that require the most background to understand. Perhaps that's why they're so commonly misunderstood. I had a lot of questions, and there weren't always easy answers. But there were always answers if I was willing to look.

That's the most important insight I can give you regarding the teachings of the Church: they may not make sense at first, but they do make sense. When I dug deep enough and consulted the right experts, I found answers for everything I doubted. And not just so-so answers but real answers that convinced me that this was truth. The Catholic faith is reasonable. It makes sense. You may think it doesn't, but I would say that's because you haven't looked closely enough. If you study with an open mind, I guarantee you will find truth that satisfies your curiosity and soothes your soul.

WHY IS SOME SOIL MORE FERTILE?

I would say that the Rosary, Sunday Mass, eucharistic adoration, and theological study are essentials for growing in faith and making your soul fertile ground to receive God's Word. We don't still do all of these. Devotions come and go. And that's okay. The point is, whenever something good came along, we said yes. Whenever there was another step to take, we took it. Whenever we found out about something that could help, we were open to it.

Why are some hearts more fertile than others? Because those people say yes to God. How do you go further after you've cleared the obstacles? Say yes! Wherever God is leading you, say yes. Whatever it is you feel God calling you to—do it. Take that leap. Be generous. Be receptive to whatever God is moving you toward and whatever his will is for you. Say yes to him, and he will make your heart fertile ground.

REFLECT

How often do you say yes to God? When you have a feeling he's calling you to take up a new devotion, volunteer for a ministry, or join a class or study group, do you act? Or do you make excuses and refuse? God needs you. He wants to use you to build up his kingdom. He's calling you to be more active and to cooperate with him in changing the world. Do you want to answer the call? Will you say yes to God?

PRAY

In your prayer today, reflect on your devotional life and ask God if you need to add some devotions to help you grow in faith. Ask God which practices would be most beneficial for you, and listen for what he tells you. Once you figure out what he's calling you to, say yes.

LIVE

The devotional practices I mention here aren't just for those who feel they've "arrived." In fact, the exact opposite is true. It was these devotional practices that helped my wife and me over-come our obstacles. We implemented these practices slowly over the course of six to eight months, many of them before we were completely "in" with the Church. Don't wait until you've arrived—start today! Pick one devotion and commit to doing it regularly for at least thirty days. Ask God to help you keep your commitment. After it becomes an ingrained part of your life, add another and continue. Then make these into family devotions and slowly incorporate your children into the mix. They won't be able to do as much as you, but they'll be doing it, and that's the key.

PART III
WHAT KIND
OF EDUCATION
FOSTERS FAITH?

Part I examines how faith works, establishes that religious education programs aren't enough to build the lasting faith children need, and touches on the great faith formation potential of families. Part II covers how to open your own heart to faith in God and cultivate that faith. So what can you do to instill faith in your children that will last?

You need to establish two things. First, you need to convey an understanding of Catholicism that leads to faith. In chapter 3, I criticize the abstract, fact-focused knowledge that's often found in parish religious education programs. However, there's another way of presenting theology that leads to an appreciation of the depth, symmetry, and cohesiveness of the Catholic faith. This is the subject of this third part of the book. Second, you need to create a daily environment in which faith is actively lived and rewarded. I cover that in part IV.

The following chapters highlight four elements that are essential to a greater understanding of Jesus Christ and deeper devotion to him. If I could design a religious education program, it would be built around these four elements: the story of salvation; the Bible; the liturgy, especially the Mass; and adult mentoring relationships.

The last one is a bit out of place because it's not strictly an educational element; however, the mentoring relationship is the glue that holds everything together.

The approach I propose is more supplementing than replacing the formal parish religious education program. Unless you have a homeschooled family, you probably don't have time to do a full-on, systematic religious education curriculum with your children. But supplementing what your children receive at the parish with these four home-based educational elements will produce lasting effects on their faith lives. Becoming knowledgeable about these four elements in order to teach them to your kids will have a huge effect on your own faith life as well.

9.
UNDERSTANDING THE STORY OF SALVATION

We all love things that are organized and well designed, even if we're not organized ourselves and perhaps especially if we're not designers. That's why the HGTV shows with incredible design makeovers are so popular. We watch professionals turn chaos into order, unsightliness into beauty. When they're done with a house, everything looks just right and fits together perfectly. It's organized and it works, and that's appealing.

My grandmother loved large jigsaw puzzles—I mean the really large ones with more than two thousand pieces. She did them on a table in the living room. Of course, no one in the family could resist trying to fit in a piece or two when they passed by the table. When you see something in pieces that's supposed to be whole, you can't help but try to put it together. That's just how people are wired. We like things organized.

The interesting thing was that any one of us, without any prior experience of a particular puzzle, could sit down in front of the pile of pieces and just start working. Why? Because there was a picture on the top of the box that showed what the completed puzzle was supposed to look like. The cover picture was our guide.

The Catholic faith can feel kind of like a large jigsaw puzzle. We learn the pieces—commandments, sacraments, doctrines—but we can't see how they fit together. Wouldn't it be great if there were a cover picture that served as a guide for the Catholic faith? Well, there is! But it's not an image; it's a story—the *story of salvation*. Catholicism is a unified, connected whole. All the pieces fit together and are organized around this central story. However, if you don't know the story, you can't see the connections. The faith seems like a pile of puzzle pieces that don't fit together. And that rankles.

When something isn't organized, especially information, most people just drop it in frustration and move onto the next thing. That's why it's so vitally important to give your children a central, organizing theme for fitting all the doctrinal puzzle pieces together. This story and its connections will prove invaluable in helping your children not only comprehend the inner logic and beauty of the Catholic faith but fall in love with it. But in order to tell the story of salvation to your children, you first need to understand it yourself.

WHAT IS THE STORY OF SALVATION?

The story of salvation, also known as *salvation history*, is the story of God and his relationship with humanity. It tells how God created and loved mankind and nurtured humanity to spiritual maturity. It tells how mankind has journeyed from godly riches to slavery and back again, and how the hero-king, the rescuer Jesus Christ, came down from his throne to share his life and deliver us from captivity. Quite literally, salvation history is the story of how we are saved—of our redemption in Jesus Christ. But it's much more than that: it's the picture on the puzzle box, the framework for understanding who you are in this world and what you're meant to be.

We understand salvation history primarily from the Bible. The Bible is a collection of writings with different literary forms, including poetry, prayers, proverbs, letters, and narratives. In particular, the narrative books tell a story that unfolds over thousands of years . . . and it all fits together.

The story begins with creation, Adam and Eve, their original sin, and their fall from grace. Jesus Christ is at the heart of the story; he is the interpretive key. All of salvation history centers on Jesus and his sacrifice on the Cross. Everything before his birth leads to him. Everything after his death emanates from him.

But there is also a backstory that begins before creation, and you can't understand it without understanding one more essential piece—the Trinity. Before time and creation, God lived and loved in a union of Persons so perfect and wonderful it can't really be described. God created us to live in this union with him; everything God has done is for that purpose—the union of mankind to himself in a never-ending torrent of divine love.

The story of salvation is a true story. The historical narrative of the Bible is not a fairy tale or something made up for the purpose of analogy. It really happened. God writes the world's history the way men write books: he crafts the actual events of history in the same way an author crafts words and organizes chapters. He arranges events so that, from the dawn of time, history is telling a story—his story.

THE POWER OF TYPOLOGY

Knowing the underlying story of the Bible is important for getting the big picture of Catholicism, but the most powerful aid to understanding is *typology*, a way of interpreting the Bible that emphasizes connections within the story. Think about how authors throw in little details at the beginning of a story that hint at what will happen in the end. It's a literary device, called *foreshadowing*, that helps the reader make connections and better understand the story. Typology shows how the New Testament is foreshadowed in the Old, which helps explain what Jesus is saying and doing. Additionally, the Old Testament is only fully revealed and made understandable in light of the New.

Typology enthralled me and led to my love affair with the Catholic faith. Typology is not a new way of understanding the Bible; it's actually how the early Church formulated her essential beliefs. I first learned about typology from popular Catholic speaker and biblical theologian Scott Hahn. He pointed out amazing connections within the Bible that I had never heard before. They explained so much.

Here's an example: In Genesis God tells Abraham to take his beloved son Isaac with him to Mount Moriah to sacrifice him as he would a lamb. That foreshadows God the Father's sacrifice of his only beloved son Jesus on Calvary. God intervenes and rescues Isaac from the hand of death, pointing us to the Resurrection, where God the Father raises his beloved son from death.

Here's another one: The Jewish Passover celebration is a memorial of God having saved the nation of Israel from slavery in Egypt. God sent the tenth plague to kill all the firstborn in Egypt, but the Israelites were spared through sacrificing a lamb and painting its blood on their doorposts as a sign for the plague to "pass over" their houses. This foreshadows Jesus's sacrificing himself as the Lamb of God during a Passover celebration. His death becomes the New Passover as he saves humanity from the slavery of sin and death through the shedding of his blood.

Typology also sheds light on Catholic beliefs about the Blessed Mother. Protestants look at her small showing in the New Testament and wonder what all the Catholic fuss is about. But the Church doesn't formulate doctrinal understanding from the New

Testament alone. It takes into account the unity and content of the whole Bible and the oral Tradition that gave birth to it. From this perspective, every strong woman in the Bible prefigures and fore-shadows Mary and gives meaning to her role.

For instance, in the court of the Davidic kings, there was an official position for the mother of the king; she was called the *gebirah*, or queen mother. Ancient Israelite kings made political alliances through marriages, so they sometimes had several hundred wives. Who was the queen? If the king chose one from among his wives, he would have huge problems. But he had only one mother. This foreshadows Mary as Queen of Heaven. She's the queen mother and has a special place in heaven because she is the Mother of Jesus.

PUTTING THE PIECES OF CATHOLICISM TOGETHER

Salvation history and typology debunk the common misconception that Catholicism is random, primitive, and irrational. Nothing could be further from the truth. The Catholic faith is a sophisticated, unified network of signs and concepts that mutually interpret each other. It's logical, organized, and reasonable.

Doctrine explains the "what" of Catholicism, but the story of salvation explains the "why"—the "so what?" and the "now what?" That's essential. It's not enough to know what to do; you need to understand why you're doing it and where it's leading you. People tend to reject a message if those two elements aren't clear.

For me, salvation history and typology brought order and sense to many pieces of Catholicism. These two ways of examining the history of our faith communicated the wisdom, passion, and profound meaning of beliefs that I once considered dull and lifeless.

They showed me that God has a plan, that he is not random in the least. I saw that if he could orchestrate all these details over thousands of years to fit perfectly together, then he surely had me figured into the mix as well. I was planned. I was wanted. I was loved into existence with a purpose. I am not random, unnecessary, or insignificant. I am known and cherished, and there is a place for me for all eternity in my Father's house.

Understanding salvation history is essential to understanding who we are as human persons. It sheds clarifying light on the mystery of the human condition. This is not just God's story, it's your story, too . . . your family story. The story of salvation is like your family genealogy. It tells you where you came from and who you are. It explains why you have longings you don't understand and how you can fill the restlessness in your heart. You're made for union with God, your Father, and only in him will you find rest.

REFLECT

What is your understanding of Catholicism? Do the beliefs of the Catholic Church seem like a pile of puzzle pieces that don't fit together? Are there doctrines that don't make sense to you? Do you struggle to find meaning in the Catholic faith? Are you ready to do some studying?

PRAY

In prayer today, ponder the magnitude of God's love as well as the beauty and symmetry of his plan of salvation. Ask the Lord to give you an appreciation of the inner unity, interconnectedness, and logic of salvation history. Also, ask God for the motivation to study and learn this saving truth in order to pass it on to your children.

LIVE

My "go-to" authority on salvation history is Scott Hahn. He has books on the sacraments, the Church, Mary, confession, angels, and Catholic traditions, all of which he approaches from a typological perspective. I recommend starting with his first book, *A Father Who Keeps His Promises*. It organizes salvation history into six stages that culminate with Jesus establishing the Catholic Church. It's easy to read and understand and will give you the basic outline of the story of salvation.

Hahn also has a free online study, called *Covenant Love: Introducing the Biblical Worldview*, that details the significant typological connections in salvation history. You can find it at salvationhistory.com. Another great resource from Hahn's apostolate, the St. Paul Center for Biblical Theology, is *Breaking the Bread*, a free monthly newsletter that includes Sunday Mass reading commentaries with a typological perspective.

I also recommend the Great Adventure Bible Study series published by Ascension Press. These are video-based studies featuring Jeff Cavins, a former evangelical pastor who came back to the Catholic faith after leaving as a teen. They are more expensive and require an investment of time but are well worth the money and the effort. Cavins is an exceptional teacher and a highly engaging speaker. You should start with *The Bible Timeline*, a twenty-four-week study that takes you through the same covenant structure as *A Father Who Keeps His Promises* but in greater detail. In addition to the video presentations by Cavins, you get a Bible reading plan and study materials that help you draw out the important lessons from the biblical text.

For your children, Ascension Press offers a salvation history study called The Great Adventure Kids. It has the same structure as the adult studies but is geared toward younger kids. For older children, there is a shorter, middle school version of the timeline called Encounter and a high school version titled T3: The Teen Timeline. I highly recommend doing the children's study and watching the video programs with your children when they're old enough.

10.
LEARNING THE STORY THROUGH THE BIBLE

The last chapter implies but does not directly state an important truth: in the end, the Catholic religion is not primarily a systematized set of doctrines. It is a story. While some rules, legislation, and codification are necessary, the heart of Catholicism is this tale of redemption, the unbelievable true story of what God has done to save us from sin and eternal separation from his love.

Why then do educators insist on teaching the faith as a list of facts instead of a narrative of salvation? Stories are hands down the simplest, most effective way of passing on information . . . especially to kids. Stories are structured, engaging, and memorable. We are storytelling creatures: history began with human beings telling stories.

There is no better way to learn Catholicism than to learn it as a story—the story of salvation—and the best way for your kids to learn that story is by reading the Bible. The Bible is God's revelation of the content of the story. Reading it as a connected whole illuminates the unity of God's plan for ourselves and all mankind. I know the idea of getting your kids reading the Bible sounds daunting. In the last section of this chapter, I introduce a plan I developed over several years of trial and error that got my kids into the habit of reading the Bible daily. And they actually like it . . .

most of the time. It isn't complicated, and I'm sure you'll be able to use it, too.

THE BIBLE: TELLING
THE STORY OF SALVATION

Read your Bible. This phrase strikes a chord of fear in most Catholics. As a whole, we Catholics don't have a good track record with reading the Bible. Most of us have little or no experience reading the Bible. It's not part of Catholic culture and definitely not a huge part of our religious education system. It's not discouraged, just not emphasized. But the Bible is Catholic! And believe it or not, Catholics are (traditionally, at least) Bible Christians.

My own devotional Bible reading has fluctuated over the years—sometimes consistent, other times nonexistent. When I came back to the Church, I tried reading the Old Testament, but it made no sense to me, and some of the stories were just strange. Then I tried reading St. Paul. He was a little better but also confusing. I found out that it's essential to have a guide for your reading—once the structure of the story of salvation lights the way, your Bible reading will have a lot more clarity.

It's not merely a convenient coincidence that the Bible is the best way of teaching the basics of the Catholic faith. The biblical authors understood that Christian revelation is essentially a story, so they set about telling it. Look at the opening paragraph of the apostle John's first letter:

> We declare to you what was from the beginning, what
> we have heard, what we have seen with our eyes, what
> we have looked at and touched with our hands, concern-
> ing the word of life—this life was revealed, and we have
> seen it and testify to it, and declare to you the eternal life
> that was with the Father and was revealed to us—we

> declare to you what we have seen and heard so that you
> also may have fellowship with us; and truly our fellow-
> ship is with the Father and with his Son Jesus Christ.
> (1 Jn 1:1–3)

John says it plainly: he wants to lead his reader to union with God through telling the story of his experiences with Jesus. In the New Testament, you get a peek at how the apostles instructed the early Church in the Catholic faith. They expounded God's miraculous dealings with mankind in history and explained how Jesus fulfilled them. This is especially true of St. Paul, who starts with a Jewish history lesson whenever he wants to lay a foundation for further explanation.

THE WAY IT'S ALWAYS BEEN DONE

The New Testament is, in fact, a written record of how the apostles taught the early Church about Jesus and the implications of his coming. The four gospels—Matthew, Mark, Luke, and John—not only tell the story of Jesus, but illuminate how the Old Testament is fulfilled in Jesus and what that means if you believe in him. Likewise, the Acts of the Apostles and the letters of St. Paul and the other apostles are expositions on how we should live in light of Christ's coming. Finally, Revelation lays out what our final end will be since Christ came in the flesh and effected our salvation.

The great teachers of the early Church adopted the same methodology. When asked how one should begin teaching the Christian faith, St. Augustine responded, "We should begin our narration, starting out from the fact that God made all things very good, and continuing . . . down to the present period of Church history."[1] Obviously, you have to skip a few details. How do you know what to include? You include the events that "converge upon the coming of Christ," writes Augustine, while always keeping in mind "that he to whom you speak by hearing may believe, and by believing may hope, and by hoping may love."[2] In other words, concentrate on the typological connections between the Old and New Testaments that relate to our salvation and that lead to active faith.

To summarize, here are the reasons the Bible is essential for teaching your children about Catholicism and leading them to faith:

1. Stories are the best way to learn things, and since Christian revelation is basically a story, Christianity lends itself to storytelling.

2. The Bible tells the story of Christian revelation—the story of salvation.

3. The apostles spread the Gospel from the beginning through this sort of storytelling. Their essential teaching is recorded in the New Testament.

4. Following the example of the apostles, the early Church Fathers taught the Christian faith this way, as well.

HOW TO GET YOUR KIDS READING THE BIBLE

My children started regular Bible reading as part of a family catechesis program I implemented at my parish. In this program, kids turned in the number of minutes they read each month and we gave them prizes. There was also an award at the end of the year for the highest totals. To tell you the truth, I had never thought about having my kids read the Bible before then—it seemed like too much for them. But how would it have looked if the kids of the guy running the program hadn't read anything? So I basically came up with this plan out of desperation.

FIRST STEP: YOU READ TO THEM

At first, it was easy. They were too young to read. I could, however, read to them and count the minutes. So I did. At night, before they went to bed, we read Bible stories. I started with children's storybook Bibles. These Bibles told stories of major players like Noah, Moses, Abraham, and David in the Old Testament, and of course Jesus in the New. When we finished one Bible, we'd start another. I used both Catholic and Protestant Bibles, as there were no major differences at this level, but distinctions begin to matter as the children get older.

You'll want to think about progressively initiating your children into the story of salvation—overlaying the central narrative of our salvation on top of the picturesque episodes in storybook Bibles. Obviously, this will correspond to your children's ages. Detail is not important in the beginning. In the lower grades, you want to get the basic story line in place. You don't need to worry about abstractions; just deal in the concrete. You're building a foundational framework on which you can hang greater details and doctrines later.

As my kids got older, I moved up to reading them longer story Bibles with more stories and more detail. I continued to revisit the sweeping story of salvation, adding more detail as appropriate. Talk with someone on your parish staff about solid biblical resources for children, visit a local Catholic bookstore if you have one, or search online for Catholic Bible resources.

NEXT STEP: THEY READ TO THEMSELVES

Hold on to those story Bibles even after you've read them to your kids several times. When your children start reading, these Bibles will be at the perfect level. Start them with the simplest ones and work your way up.

Once we established the routine of reading the Bible at bedtime, it wasn't too hard getting them to read on their own. We had been doing it for years. I set a goal of five minutes every night. That doesn't sound like much, right? You'll probably be tempted to ask for more. Don't. Five minutes is plenty, especially in the beginning. I firmly believe in the concept of *microhabits*—tiny changes that pay big dividends over time. Five minutes is not taxing, it's not a hard sell, and it adds up. Of course, they could read more if they wanted to. Often they did.

You do have to check up on them. We were recording minutes for the program, so my kids had to log what they read every night. I would ask if they were reading and pop in from time to time to catch them in the act. I would also ask them questions and engage in discussions about the stories they were reading, making sure to reinforce their understanding of salvation history.

FINAL STEP: THEY GRADUATE TO A REAL BIBLE

When they outgrew the story Bibles, perhaps around fifth grade, I got them real Bibles. I started with paraphrase translations like *The Good News Bible*. Some disagree and think kids should have a "real" Bible, like the *New American Bible*. I think the best Bible is the one that will actually get read. If the language is too literal and stuffy, kids will be turned off and reading will become a chore. You don't want that. Catholics are notorious for having beautiful, leather-bound Bibles that look great and never get read. Don't get your kids a keepsake that looks good on a shelf. Get them a Bible they'll use and enjoy, whether it be a paraphrase or a "real" Bible.

* * *

So there's my plan. It worked great with my kids. I started when they were very young, and they're still reading the Bible every night as teenagers. They really know the story line of the Bible now and have even delved into some tough Old Testament books like Kings, although the violence was too much at times when they were younger. Over the years, they've built up quite a bit of Bible knowledge. I'm often surprised by how much they know and understand.

REFLECT

What's your attitude toward the Bible? Do you see it as vital to your spiritual life? Have you ever tried reading it? Have you ever thought about praying with the Bible daily? There are great spiritual benefits of daily Bible reading and prayer. Catholics tend to think of this as a Protestant thing and shy away from it. However, praying with the Bible is actually an ancient Catholic practice called *lectio divina*, or "divine reading."

The Bible is God's Word. It is living and active. The Holy Spirit can work through the words to inspire you, solve problems, answer questions, or simply touch your heart with God's love. It takes some practice, but praying with the Bible can be amazingly fruitful.

Two good books on the subject are *Lectio Divina: An Ancient Prayer That Is Ever New* by Mario Masini and *Sacred Reading: The Ancient Art of Lectio Divina* by Michael Casey. Both are excellent. Masini succinctly breaks down the method and is more instructive. Casey is a slightly harder read but delves into the background, history, and theory, which is well worth the effort. Lectio divina is a phenomenal practice and one of my favorite ways to pray. It will revolutionize your prayer life.

PRAY

Try praying with the Bible (lectio divina) today. Say a short vocal prayer asking the Holy Spirit to be with you. Read a short passage and then think about it. What's happening in the passage? Does anything stand out to you? What do you find interesting? How does it relate to you spiritually? Tell God any thoughts, feelings, or desires you have, and then spend time in silence listening. Make a resolution to act on any intuitions or insights you receive. Finally, thank God and end by praying an Our Father.

LIVE

You can do a modified lectio divina with your kids. I did this all the time when I was reading to my boys. After they started reading to themselves, we did Bible reading/lectio at special times. There are even some children's Bibles that are built around it.

First, as you read, ask them what's going on in the passage. What is happening? What is Jesus saying? How are the other persons in the passage relating to him? What is their attitude toward him? Get your kids to reflect on the passage and add your own thoughts as well.

Next, draw out the lesson in the passage. What does this say to you? What does it mean for you? Is there something we can learn from Jesus in this passage? Find the application to your children's lives, and your own life, and talk about it. You might take this opportunity to make some of the big-picture, typological connections introduced in the last chapter. It's quite possible those will aid in understanding the application of the passage.

Then, formulate a prayer based on the application you discussed. You might ask for help implementing the lesson. Perhaps you ask forgiveness for the behavior you identified. Maybe you just pray to be closer to Jesus. Finally, discuss how you might act on this new insight or start this new behavior.

11.
EXPERIENCING THE STORY IN THE LITURGY

The goal of faith formation is not a theoretical knowledge of Catholic doctrine, but a lived experience of faith in Jesus Christ. Christian revelation is essentially a story, and that story provides the underlying context for everything Catholic. The story of salvation not only demystifies Catholic doctrine but is the perfect vehicle for delivering that doctrine. Regular Bible reading puts you vividly in touch with the story and brings it to life.

The story of salvation is not just history. It emanates from the past and forms our present. The Jesus you meet and get to know in the Bible is alive and active in the world, not a dead figure from long ago. Through the Holy Spirit, Jesus lives in you and acts through you. He works to communicate his holiness to you. How does this sharing of Christ's divine life happen? Through the *liturgy*.

WHAT IS LITURGY?

When most of us think of liturgy, we think of Mass. (I know, you think Mass is boring and it's hard to take your kids when they're young. However, you'll think different once you understand the importance, and power, of liturgy.) The Mass is a liturgy and that's where we most often experience it, but liturgy encompasses far more. Baptisms, Confirmations, and other sacramental celebrations are also part of the Church's liturgy. The Liturgy of the Hours, or Divine Office—a set of Bible readings, psalms, and prayers said every day by priests and religious—extends the Mass and is also part of the church's liturgy. And, the feast days and holy days that ornament the seasons of the Church's liturgical year are aspects of liturgy, as well. These unfold the mystery of salvation throughout the year and draw the minds of the faithful toward God.

Liturgy is where the work of our redemption takes place. Through the interaction of signs, symbols, and words in liturgical celebrations, Christ dispenses to us the grace he won on the Cross. An ocean of grace flowed out into the world through the redemptive self-offering of Jesus, but it doesn't do us any good just floating out there in space. The way this grace reaches us is through the sacramental liturgy. Grace is God's own life poured into our souls, giving us power for living as Christians.

Liturgy presents concrete expressions of faith for children and, like a seal on wax, makes lasting impressions. Seasons, special celebrations, incense, statues, colors—these tangible elements of liturgy make the faith incarnate. Liturgy makes faith sensory, and that's important because we are sensorial beings. Your children experience the world not only through their minds and imaginations but through their bodies. Catholicism has a fantastic ability to give material utterance to the immaterial and thus make it real. The Catholic practice of faith takes humanness into account at every turn, incorporating it into our praise of God.

It's safe to say that the "smells and bells" of Catholic worship were a large part of Shannon's and my coming back to the Catholic Church. Originally, Catholic thought drew us back, but for a brief time we wondered whether we should explore other churches. In the end, we figured we might as well stay Catholic because we already knew what to *do*! Having grown up Catholic, I knew all the rituals and nuances of Catholic life. It was a little like coming home. Shannon had fond memories of the beautiful church she had attended with her family as a girl. She recalled feeling awash with peace when praying before a statue of Mary at a particularly difficult time in her childhood. I was surprised and pleased to still be able to recite the Mass responses after all those years, especially the Nicene Creed. I was still an insider, one of the gang . . . and it felt good. All those Catholic ways of praying and worshipping God had taken root in us because our whole beings were engaged. Deep in our bones we remained Catholic, despite years of dormant faith.

Liturgy is decisively important for faith formation. It is an excellent teaching tool because it contains and makes familiar the heart of the story of salvation. You can talk and look at pictures all day, but the liturgy is tangible. It's a giant object lesson on the tale of our redemption. The statues, stained glass, symbols, changing vestment and altar colors, church decorations, and swinging incense holders—those "smells and bells"—all express the faith in concrete, sometimes dramatic ways, recalling salvation history and making the past a present reality. To get the most out of liturgy, you'll need to concentrate on two elements: the liturgical year and the Mass.

THE STORY OF SALVATION LIVED THROUGH THE LITURGICAL YEAR

The liturgical year divides the Church calendar into five seasons: Advent, Christmas, Lent, Easter, and Ordinary Time. Each season has a different emphasis, from somber penance to glorious celebration. Certain days, called feast days, are reserved to commemorate and celebrate important events in the life of Jesus, the role of Mary in the Church, and particular mysteries of the faith such as the Body and Blood of Christ, the Blessed Trinity, and the Nativity of Christ. There are also feast days that celebrate the lives of saints.

Structuring Church worship and devotion by season is brilliant because it takes into account how we live and operate as humans. We all love seasons. Think of the excitement and anticipation that builds toward holidays such as Thanksgiving and Christmas or how your activities change with the seasonal changes in weather. The same dynamic takes place within the liturgical year: different liturgical seasons have different emphases. If you do the same thing all the time, eventually it grows stale and loses significance. You couldn't maintain the somber, penitential practice of Lent all year long, but for forty days you can buckle down, do penance, and work on ridding yourself of faults. Likewise, you wouldn't want the festive, joy-filled atmosphere of Christmas year-round. You'd get sick of it. But it's energizing and exciting for a while.

Every year the Church relives the story of our redemption in Christ through the liturgical seasons. The two greatest celebrations of the year, Christmas and Easter, center on his coming and his salvific sacrifice. The liturgy is Christocentric—centered on Christ—and typological.

In Advent, the preparatory season before Christmas, we assume the anticipation of ancient Israel waiting long, interminable centuries for the Messiah to come. At Advent Masses, the Old Testament readings are intimately connected with the New Testament gospel readings, evoking the panoply of messianic prophecies and their fulfillment in the person of Jesus.

The same holds true for Lent. The interplay of Old and New Testament readings during this season illuminates the true nature of Jesus's mission as the Suffering Servant who sacrifices himself for the sin of the nations. The readings relentlessly lead us toward the Passion and Christ's triumph at Easter. The Easter Vigil Mass is the high point of the liturgical year. Seven Old Testament readings with accompanying psalms lead us through salvation history to its climax: the gospel account of Mary Magdalene and friends at the empty tomb—the Resurrection. No one participating in this liturgy with attention and an open heart can help but be instructed in the basic Christian message and the very core of Catholic belief.

THE GRACES OF SALVATION COMMUNICATED THROUGH THE MASS

The Mass has a unique quality: it not only presents salvation history, but gives what it teaches. Every sacramental celebration recalls elements of the story of salvation while applying the particular effects of that sacrament. For example, at a Baptism, the priest blesses the baptismal water with a prayer that recounts the times in salvation history when water was used to create or save life (creation, the flood, Moses at the Red Sea). These Old Testament events prefigure our redemption through Baptism and at the same time explain what's happening to the person being baptized through the power of the Holy Spirit. The sacraments both present the story of salvation and let us immediately participate in it.

With no sacrament is this truer than with the Eucharist. In the Eucharistic Prayer, the priest prays aloud our shared thanksgiving for the wonder of our salvation. He then recounts in particular detail the Last Supper narrative. It's almost as though we are there. We're all gathered around a table, the priest takes bread and wine, and he says the same words Jesus said—even in the first person. He prays a blessing over the bread and wine, calling upon the Holy Spirit to sanctify our gifts. By the power of the Holy Spirit, bread and wine become the Body and Blood of Christ. The sacrifice of the Cross is made present, re-presented, and we become a part of it. All of the saving action contained in Christ's Passion— the outpouring of love to the Father, the redemptive self-sacrifice, the tidal wave of re-creating grace—comes into us through our reception of Christ's Body and Blood. Salvation history plays out around us: we become a part of God's action in it, and he applies its saving grace to us.

Unfortunately, mere attendance at Mass doesn't guarantee a transformational experience. If you can't read the signs, the liturgy won't have much effect on you. Thousands, if not millions, of Catholics attend Mass completely oblivious to the spiritual reality of what's happening around them. The story of salvation provides the framework that makes sense of all the people, places, and particular stories found in the Bible. You have to unlock the liturgy, for yourself first and then for your children, so your family can appreciate and participate in it fully.

REFLECT

Is Mass a chore for you? Do you go to Mass on Sunday but dread it? Do you know you're supposed to go but lack the motivation to get there? I want to challenge you to study what liturgy and the Mass are all about. Once you truly understand what's happening, Mass will never be dull for you again. Two resources can help you here. The first is *Celebrating the Mass: A Guide for Understanding and Loving the Mass More Deeply* by Alfred McBride. This booklet will help you understand everything that's happening in the Mass. Analyzing all the parts and responses, McBride gives an in-depth explanation of the history, theology, and symbolism. I read *Celebrating the Mass* every year while preparing my RCIA candidates for Easter, and every year my faith is renewed as I am reminded of the richness and profound beauty of the eucharistic sacrifice.

My other recommendation is a book by Scott Hahn called *The Lamb's Supper*. Drawing from Old Testament prophets and Revelation, it illuminates a typological understanding of the Mass. You'll learn about the invisible spiritual reality that surrounds you at

Mass and about what happens in heaven every time we celebrate Mass here on earth. I meet people all the time who came back to the Church because of this book. It's a game changer.

PRAY

Next time you go to Mass, ponder the greatness of what's happening around you. Jesus is present, offering himself for the salvation of the world. Angels adore, earth joins to heaven, and grace flows out to heal your wounded heart. Thank the Lord for his mercy. Open your heart and invite Jesus to enter there fully.

LIVE

Help your children understand how the story of salvation unfolds over the course of the liturgical year. You should celebrate the great feast days together as a family and train your children from an early age to understand them within the context of salvation history, especially Christmas, Holy Week, and Easter. You can do this through activities and Bible reading.

Christmas is a great example. Of course, you won't have any problem celebrating Christmas, but you can't stop at Santa and gift giving. Dive into the Christian meaning of Christmas by preparing during Advent. Traditional props like Advent wreaths and calendars highlight the events and invite children to count down the days leading up to Christ's birth. The Jesse Tree is a craft-friendly, interactive lesson highlighting the genealogy of Jesus. Every day you learn how different Old Testament characters foreshadow Jesus's life and mission.

Our family adores this series of entertaining historical fiction books written by Arnold Ytreeide that is set in the time leading up to Jesus' birth. The first, titled *Jotham's Journey*, is about a shepherd boy, Jotham, who loses his family at the time of the Roman census and must get to Bethlehem to find them. Along the way, you relive the Christmas story as Jotham has many adventures and meets characters (some fictional, some historical) associated with the Infancy Narratives of the gospels. Subsequent books in the series interweave stories in the same setting from the perspective of the different characters Jotham met.

During Advent, the Mass readings take advantage of how Old Testament prophecy is mated to New Testament Gospel fulfillment in Christ and should form the basis of your Bible reading. These readings reveal the true nature of the season; familiarity with them will deepen your children's liturgical experience at Mass on Christmas Day. Lent and Easter are similarly rich seasons for activities that weave together salvation history, Bible readings, and liturgy.

Liturgical celebrations of feasts clarify and emphasize the most important theological concepts of our salvation, including Mary as Mother of God, the institution of the Eucharist, the Resurrection, Pentecost, the Body and Blood of Christ, and the Assumption of the Blessed Virgin. But before your children even understand the concepts, they should experience them as living, concrete truths that are part of their lives. The feasts are not just history; they make the historical events live today. Think of a birthday celebration. We recount and give thanks for what happened in the past so that our present is changed somehow. So, too, at Mass, Christ is actively working through the liturgy to change us today, to make us holy. He's not just the Jesus of history but, as St. Paul says, "Christ in you, the hope of glory" (Col 1:27).

The calendar of saints' feast days is another important aspect of the liturgical year. From the beginning this was central to Shannon's daily devotions, and early on she began sharing it with our boys. There are numerous books at all age levels that give short biographies of the saints on their feast days. Every morning at breakfast, Shannon reads aloud to us about the saint of the day.

The saints give us concrete examples of people who got it right. They are the witnesses that holiness is possible. Their testimony powerfully inspires us, teaches us the Christian life, and shows us the joy and hope that comes from living in union with God.

12.
DEVELOPING MENTORING RELATIONSHIPS

We've explored three of the educational elements that go into forming a vibrant, faith-filled understanding of Catholicism. The story of salvation provides the framework and system for organizing and categorizing what seems like a large amount of unrelated theological detail. The Bible reveals the content of the story. The liturgy is the means of enacting the story within each of us by recalling God's actions and, through the power of the Holy Spirit working in the sacraments, applies the saving effects of those actions to our lives today.

One final piece is missing: mentoring relationships. Knowledge is one thing; translating it into action is another. It's absolutely necessary to know the truths of the faith, but knowledge alone is not motivation to live them. Relationship makes faith formation work—if you miss this, everything else you do will be ineffective.

THE FOUNDATION OF FAITH TRANSMISSION

I give parish religious education programs a lot of flak for being ineffective, but in truth they're square pegs trying to fit into round holes. The classroom is a bad model for faith formation. Once a week, teachers face large groups of students they don't know and who don't know them. They deliver information but have no influence, which is what truly matters. We're not talking about academics and test scores; we're talking about life. Changed behavior, not increased knowledge, is our goal.

Contrast this with the model of mentorship. A mentor has just a few students, maybe even only one. His students spend a lot of time with him; they know him intimately and trust him implicitly. Jesus taught thousands at a time, but he formed only a few. There were twelve in his inner circle and, even within this small group, he shared everything with only three. Jesus was a mentor, and he is our perfect guide for how to spread faith.

Strong mentoring relationships are just as important as techniques and methods for effective faith formation—faith is never transmitted in a vacuum. Earning trust is the crucial first step in the process of bringing others to faith. Most people miss this, assuming that the conveyance of information is enough to touch hearts and change minds. You first have to earn the right to be heard. That goes for spreading the faith to anyone, not just children. Religion is not all in the mind, and decisions are rarely made according to reason alone. Rather, emotion and intuition are vital aspects of the decision to believe. If you don't establish a relationship of trust first, you're just a talking head and your message gets lost. To be effective, sharing faith also requires sharing yourself—opening your life and exposing yourself in a way that communicates faith. Relationship is the medium for the message. The human connections you make are like a bridge on which the divine can travel.

One of the reasons parents are particularly well suited for the ongoing faith formation of their children is that trust is already an integral component in their relationship. You've already built trust by caring for every aspect of their natural lives; why shouldn't that care extend to their spiritual lives? As we saw in chapter 4, parental relationships are the single greatest influence on children.

I'm asking you to take that relationship one step further. Forming their faith will require you to be a good moral example. As well, to develop a meaningful, personal faith relationship with them, you will need to be open, vulnerable, and honest about your own faith journey. From years of evangelizing adults, I developed the following steps for establishing and maintaining spiritual credibility.

BE AN EXAMPLE

I can't say enough about the power of example. It's simply true that your actions communicate more than your words. If faith is not a priority in your life, it won't be in your children's. This isn't always comforting for me. I mess up all the time. I'm not extremely pious; I worry I'm too worldly. I curse too much, I drive too fast, and I've lost my temper too many times to count. Often, I fear that if my actions are the deciding factor for my kids' faith, they're doomed. But I also know that Jesus is at the heart of our family, and Shannon and I have communicated that to our boys.

Your life is the proving ground for whatever religious knowledge you hand on to your children. Your actions must back up what you're saying, or your message means nothing. If your life is a witness of the Gospel, by God's grace your children will follow your example.

BE OPEN

Who would you trust more: a woman in a commercial claiming a new laundry detergent is the best thing ever or your best friend raving about a different detergent? Obviously, you'd trust your friend. The commercial is trying to sell you detergent; your friend simply wants what's best for you, so you trust her more. People want to know who's behind a message and what they're about. What are their motivations and agendas?

Often honesty and trustworthiness, rather than status or position, allow you to act as an authority. Handing on faith requires that you be transparent about your life, your faith, and your motivations. *Transparency* literally means letting someone see right through you, letting them know who you are and what's going on inside.

As your children get older, you'll need to be increasingly open with them, or you'll come off like that laundry detergent lady when you ask them to believe in Jesus. They will begin to wonder who's behind this message, why you want them to believe, and what's in it for them. You must establish "trust points." Openness about your own life builds trust. Sharing how Catholicism changed you will motivate change in your children. If they see it in your face, they'll know it's real.

BE VULNERABLE AND HONEST

Of course, being open makes you vulnerable, and a lot of people don't like that. But vulnerability also makes you more likable and more human. In my experience, being vulnerable with your children can feel a bit strange. Generally, you're the one in charge, and they're the ones who are vulnerable. Perhaps you don't want your children to have an intimate knowledge of your life and personality. However, communicating your struggles makes the whole Christian journey more believable. It makes you more believable, too.

I have shared my personal witness often in my RCIA classes, and it works incredibly well. Students told me that the demands and lofty ideals of the Christian life sometimes seemed impossible. But when I told them stories of how I struggled and overcame sins with God's grace, admitted having difficulties with certain teachings, and related the process of how I came to believe, this helped them realize they didn't have to be perfect right away and gave them hope that it was possible.

Parents are uniquely situated for this kind of personal sharing. Children are naturally curious about their parents' lives. Knowing your history gives them a connection both to you and to their own story, their inherited past. It helps create a sense of identity and place in the world. This curiosity can work in your favor when you are sharing faith with your children.

Share stories of triumph. Tell them how you went through struggles similar to theirs and finally overcame your obstacles. It will give them hope. Be honest and tell them that you're still working on things in your own spiritual life, that you haven't mastered everything yet. Obviously, you don't want to be too forthcoming about your sins, but there are ways of sharing while remaining discreet.

A particularly problematic mindset in today's youth culture is the notion that truth is subjective and can be different for everyone; what's right is shaped by your life experience and situation. In times past, people accepted Catholic teaching on the basis of Church authority or even God's authority. Today, authority has less meaning. Needless to say, this is an obstacle to establishing a Catholic worldview.

Personal witness breaks through this. No one can argue with your experience—it's yours! If you get your kids to identify with your experience and relate to it, you have a foot in the door and have opened the possibility that your truth could belong to them someday.

FIND OTHER ADULT MENTORS

As crucial and as close as the parent-child relationship is, at times you might need a little outside help because your child needs a "second opinion." Other trusted, faithful, Catholic adults give additional examples of committed Christians serving God.

Society and the media can make the Christian life look silly and worthless. If your child lives his Christian life in isolation, it may seem like your family is just a weird anomaly. However, if your child witnesses other adults who love the Lord and want to give their time and talent to serving him, he'll more likely see it as normal. That's why sports figures who openly proclaim and live their Christian faith make such an impact. These "heroes" legitimize living differently and not following the culture's siren song of fame, wealth, and power.

Youth group is a great place to find faithful adults to provide lifestyle witness. A cool youth group leader who says the same things you do can be great positive influence, as can kids a little older than your child. One example is committed Catholic teens from the high school youth group who lead small groups in the middle school program. Or, college-age kids living faithful Catholic lives who volunteer with the high school youth group. They are a powerful witness.

REFLECT

Are you comfortable talking about your inner thoughts regarding faith? Is your life an open book, or are you more private, preferring to keep things to yourself? Do you share your history with your children, or are you more reserved about your past life? Would you be willing to make your life an example and be open and vulnerable with your children if it helped them grow in faith?

PRAY

Ask the Lord to give you courage to share more of yourself with your children and with others. In prayer, reflect on the worst thing that could happen if you were more open about your life. Would anyone think worse of you? Pray about making the sacrifice of your privacy for God and for your children's faith.

LIVE

Cardinal Newman showed that personal witness works well for sharing faith. Whenever you talk about an aspect of the faith, include a personal story. It could be why you believe in something, why you didn't believe and now do, how your thinking evolved, what the turning point was, or why you think it's important.

Reflecting aloud on your life and experiences will have a double effect: it will open your children to deeper consideration of the merits of Christian faith, and it will also greatly increase your own faith. You'll come to understand your own history, motivations, and desires. Faith, and your relationship to it, will take on a whole new meaning. I guarantee it.

Sharing a personal story is very simple. However, you can't just tell it any old way—it has to be structured for effect. Here's my technique:

1. Share an opinion, perspective, feeling, or conviction from your past that your children can identify with in their present difficulty.

2. Tell them the story of how your perspective changed.

3. Finally, tell them how this change affected or transformed you, and challenge them to consider that change in their own lives.

The story is about your personal journey from one perspective to another and how that made your life better. Basically, it illustrates the action you want them to take.

A commenter on my blog once told me about sharing his faith journey with his kids. He was a convert to Catholicism. He discussed what he believed before, his motivations for converting, and why he thought the Catholic Church was better. His kids are grown now and have strong faith lives. He credited his openness about faith as an essential factor.

PART IV
HOW DO YOU CREATE AN
ENVIRONMENT OF FAITH?

Here's where everything comes together. Chapter 4 covers four ways parents are essential for nurturing real faith in their children. Part II addresses the first way, being an example of faith. Part III deals with the second, articulating the faith in a coherent way, and the third, how faith is nurtured best in the context of relationships. In these last chapters of the book, I look at the fourth: creating a home life that supports and nourishes the practice of faith.

Several years ago, I asked parish religious education directors in my region about their biggest concern—what the one thing was that most kept them from accomplishing their mission. Without hesitation, nearly all of them pointed to parents. "The children's parents don't live the faith at home! Often they don't even take their children to Mass. How can we expect to have any influence on the kids if everything they learn at the parish is undermined in their families?" they exclaimed. I've even experienced pushback from parents over being asked to involve themselves in their children's religious education. More than once, parents told me their children were in Catholic school or parish religious education in order that they wouldn't have to be involved with it at home. In their minds, religious education was the parish's job.

But the religious educators are right. It takes more than classroom education to change attitudes and actions, and that's what we're really talking about. Faith should lead to changed lives and changed behaviors—new life in Christ. Children need other types of formation in addition to education for Christian faith to be sustainable, and parents are the only ones who can provide it.

Kids need help in developing the personal skills that lead to increased faith. The first chapter in this part deals with developing spiritual skills in general, what I call "Training in Godliness." The second and third chapters discuss two essential skills that are indispensable for growth, personal relationship with God and reflective, conversational prayer. Finally, I address your whole family's attitude toward religion, your child's relationships, and how even your home itself supports your children's growth in faith.

Formal religious education is a minuscule part of children's lives, even at a Catholic school. What happens during the other 99 percent of their lives? That's what will determine their course. In this last part, I explore what only parents can do: support their children with a Catholic lifestyle and a home that is an environment of faith.

13.
TRAINING IN GODLINESS

The first thing I want to cover is personal, spiritual skills or spiritual training. Why train to be holy? Let me answer that with another question. What was your last New Year's resolution? Did you keep it? We've all had the experience of making big, life-changing resolutions that at some point fall by the wayside. That can easily happen with your commitment to Jesus. The spirit may be willing, but the flesh is indeed weak. So what can you and your children do to stay the course? Train in godliness.

SLOW AND STEADY

Last year, I experienced the power of slow, steady training. I started a ninety-day workout program that was far beyond my ability. I was unsure if I would ever be able to do it, but I bought the program anyway. Excited, and a bit apprehensive, I began. At first, I struggled—I couldn't even complete the beginners' workout. But the program's training model set me up for success. At the beginning, the goal wasn't to complete everything; it was to learn the movements and get your body used to the exercises. That gave me permission to stink. The key was working out every day and going for small changes. Gradually, I got stronger. After a while, I could do most of the exercises, then all of them. The program had a second, more advanced phase that was even harder. Again, I thought there was no way I could complete it, but I kept going. At the start of those ninety days, I didn't believe I'd ever be strong enough to do the whole workout easily, but by the end I was. Through a slow, progressive process of training, I became able to do what I thought at first was impossible. I became a believer.

Increasingly, psychologists and productivity experts say the way to do something big is to start small. By adopting tiny habits that can be accomplished daily and don't require serious effort, you gradually and incrementally improve. That's training.

The researchers who wrote *Soul Searching* found that faith-filled teens regularly engaged in spiritual training such as Bible reading, prayer, and intentional service, and that these practices strengthened faith. "Youth should be taught to practice their faith," Smith and Denton write. This applies not only in the sense of being a "practicing Catholic," but in the sense of just plain practicing, that is "consistently working on skills, habits, and virtues in the direction of excellence in faith, analogous to musicians and athletes practicing their skills."[1]

Can you gain spiritual skills? Can you train yourself to be godly? St. Paul seems to think so. He writes to his disciple Timothy, "Train yourself in godliness, for, while physical training is of some value, godliness is valuable in every way, holding promise for both the present life and the life to come" (1 Tm 4:7–8). St. Paul suggests that Timothy engage in spiritual training that's similar to athletic training.

PRACTICE SAYING NO TO SIN

Training in godliness is meant to counteract the effects of sin in your life. If you boil it down, sin is about pride and selfishness. You selfishly do what you want because you think it's good for you, even though God says it isn't. Why is it not good? Because it leads you away from him. The goal of all the rules, commandments, and laws in the Church is to lead you to live in union with God through Jesus. If an action leads you away from God, it's sin.

Your actions determine who you are, and sin closes us in on ourselves. Over time, repeated acts of sin form ingrained habits of selfishness and pride. They shut us off from God because he demands that we make a gift of ourselves to him and to others. If you're increasingly closed in on yourself—your plans, your agendas, your way of doing things—you won't want to follow God. You won't want what he offers because it interferes with what you want.

Spiritual training is repeated acts of opening toward God that draw you out of yourself and move you toward making a gift of yourself to God and others. They are small habits repeated daily that don't take much effort but over time will transform you on the inside. Think of them as spiritual calisthenics. In the same way that pushups, leg lifts, and jumping jacks condition your muscles to perform better, so these acts condition your spiritual muscles to make you more receptive to God and his will.

There are too many practices that qualify as spiritual training to discuss here, and everyone has individual needs. Some, like prayer, adoration, regular Bible reading, and participation in faith-sharing groups, are mentioned in this book. Training could include practicing virtues like humility, generosity, kindness, and detachment. Other practices include mortifications, fasting, forgiveness, self-denial, and avoiding occasions of sin.

It's best to concentrate on just a few at a time. Remember, it's about small habits that lead to big change. If you do too much at once, you'll burn out and quit. The key is developing the habit and making it a regular part of your life.

REFLECT

Do you train in godliness? Are spiritual habits, skills, and devotions a regular part of your life? Perhaps you didn't know these were important. You always went to Mass on Sunday but didn't know there was more to being Catholic than that. Spiritual training is a foundational part of traditional Catholic spirituality. It is absolutely essential to jump-starting and maintaining a strong faith. Give some thought today as to which spiritual skills you should work on.

PRAY

In your prayer today, ask the Lord what practices you should start first. If you have any concerns about being able to teach your kids about religious practices or about finding time for them, relate those to him as well. Speak to him about your own religious practices or lack of them. Commit to doing more, and ask for help in keeping that commitment.

LIVE

Spiritual training means not only teaching your children religious practices, but also setting up systems to help your children accomplish them and probably modeling those practices yourself. Your kids probably won't decide to pray or give up bad habits out of the blue. You will have to get involved. Lent is the perfect time to introduce something like this. Everyone thinks about giving things up during this time. Instead of giving up chocolate (which is kind of useless), you can have your kids work on developing a spiritual skill.

You need to create a home environment and culture that supports spiritual training. This is definitely not something the local parish can do for you, which shows once more why you are so essential to your children's faith development.

Two excellent books on developing virtue are Donald DeMarco's *The Heart of Virtue: Lessons from Life and Literature Illustrating the Beauty of Moral Character* and Peter Kreeft's *Back to Virtue: Traditional Moral Wisdom for Modern Moral Confusion.* Both are written in a popular style and are easy to read. DeMarco includes many stories and illustrations that could be read to older children as examples of living out virtue and make excellent discussion starters. Kreeft is more theological but still quite accessible.

14.
SEEK A PERSONAL RELATIONSHIP WITH GOD

At the heart of our Catholic faith is the knowledge that God is *personal*. It's really a fundamental doctrine. God is a communion of Persons—Father, Son, and Holy Spirit—whose inner life is made up of relational love. In fact, we're persons because God is personal. We're made to be persons like him so we can share in that relational love burning inside the trinitarian union of persons.

This personal God loves us. When we lost our union with him, the Second Person of the Trinity, the Son, assumed human nature to rescue us. He sacrificed himself so we could share his life in a relationship—an intimate bond, a loving communion established in Baptism and increased with every reception of the Eucharist. United with him in this way, we're then drawn back into the communion of the Trinity.

MANY CATHOLICS DON'T KNOW A PERSONAL GOD

Why am I emphasizing that God is personal? Because many Catholics don't believe it, and that is a huge obstacle to one of the bedrocks of faith: personal relationship with God.

In her book *Forming Intentional Disciples,* Sherry Weddell presents some alarming statistics about the beliefs of Catholics. She states, "Only 60 percent of Catholics believe in a *personal* God. Twenty-nine percent said that God is an 'impersonal force.'"[1] She goes on to say that "only 48 percent of Catholics were *absolutely certain* that the God they believed in was a God with whom they could have a personal relationship."[2] She later states that those numbers decrease for younger generations and correlates the belief in a personal God with Mass attendance—in groups that don't believe in the personhood of God, fewer people attend Mass.

I have to admit, the concept of a personal God was pretty foreign to me growing up Catholic. I was encouraged to pray, but the idea of having a relationship with God never entered the picture. Also, during my reversion I was exposed to many different practices, such as Mass, confession, adoration, and praying the Rosary, but no one ever advised me to develop a personal relationship with God. Although those things do contribute to a personal relationship with him, I never considered it until I was a student at Franciscan University, where it was a large part of the culture. I found out it's part of traditional Catholic spirituality as well. For instance, personal, loving union with Jesus through prayer is at the center of Carmelite spirituality. Carmelites don't call it a personal relationship, but essentially that's what it is.

FAITH THROUGH PERSONAL ENCOUNTER WITH GOD

The real job of faith formation is facilitating encounters with God. He is the one who brings conversion. On our own, we have no power whatsoever to change anyone. In the relational support of your children, you are like a matchmaker making sure your children know God personally. You don't make conversion happen, but you connect the one who needs conversion with the one who has the power to convert.

The idea of a personal relationship flows very naturally from the story of salvation. In the Bible, conversion comes through encounters with God. In the Old Testament, God reveals himself in unique ways to major players, changing them and setting them on new courses. Think about Abraham. His life is set; he's a tribal chieftain with land, flocks, and people under his care. But God breaks into his world and shows him an alternate future. God asks Abraham to trust him and follow him to a foreign place—he doesn't even tell Abraham where—promising him blessings beyond his wildest dreams. Abraham follows, his descendants form the people of Israel, and his great faith becomes the foundation of all of Judeo-Christian belief. A similarly life-changing moment is seen when Moses encounters God in the burning bush and leaves his life of forty years as a shepherd to lead Israel out of Egypt. Later in Israel's history, David is chosen by the prophet Samuel to be the king. After he's anointed, the Holy Spirit rushes upon him, uniting him in a special way with God and changing his life forever.

You see the same sort of personal transformation through relationship in the New Testament with Jesus. Peter, James, John, Matthew the tax collector, Zacchaeus, the man born blind, and the woman at the well are all transformed by personal encounter with the Lord. They meet him, he sees into their hearts, and their lives are never the same. Part of your role as spiritual mentor is introducing your kids to God through his Son Jesus and facilitating a relationship.

Think of all those people who flocked to see Jesus while he walked around Galilee and Jerusalem. They came in search of something from him: healing, freedom from demonic possession, a new understanding of God, hope of divine assistance, or peace of heart. They had to have heard about him somehow, about the teaching, about the miracles, about the changed lives. People spread the word about this new manifestation of God in their midst. I think of those people as early spiritual mentors, facilitating encounters with Jesus, bringing people into contact with the one who could change them.

PERSONAL RELATIONSHIP WITH JESUS

In many ways, a relationship with Jesus is easier to think about than a relationship with God the Father because Jesus actually lived on earth, and one of Catholics' core beliefs is that he's alive today in heaven, with a resurrected body. We can imagine what Jesus looks like, and we know who he is from the gospels. In fact, one of the reasons regular Bible reading should be an essential spiritual practice is so that we become familiar with what he said and did. We get to know Jesus and understand him better by encountering him in the gospels. You can't have a relationship with someone you don't know. Also, the Holy Spirit can work through the words of the Bible and bring an encounter with Jesus through prayerful reading.

Jesus is the mediator between God and man, so it's right to direct our prayer and our attention to him. He's the center of everything: the sacraments, our liturgical celebrations, our worship. He's our hero, our rescuer, our savior. Actively encourage a relationship with Jesus, our older brother in the faith. Use the name of Jesus often. Direct your prayer and intercessions to him. (Beyond the obvious benefits to yourself, if you don't do this you're passing up an excellent formation opportunity.) Knowing that Jesus is with you as a companion is a powerful motivator. Jesus is the tangible expression of the infinite God's limitless love. He died on the Cross to save you. What would he not do for you? If you can grasp this, loving him and loving the Father through him become much easier.

WHAT DOES A RELATIONSHIP WITH GOD LOOK LIKE?

Part of the problem with having a relationship with God is that not many people are sure what it looks like. We understand how to have a relationship with a live person, but God is sort of out there, invisible, intangible, and, in many cases, seemingly impersonal. God's not physically standing in front of you so you can't see facial expressions or emotions or hear tone of voice or replies to your questions. But that doesn't mean there's no way to have a real friendship with the give and take of conversation. . . . It's just a little different.

A relationship with God is similar to a relationship with anyone. You spend time together, share your joys and sorrows, talk about what's on your mind, listen, respond, and react. Like any relationship, it requires certain actions that benefit the union. You have to do certain things to accommodate the other and help each other out. Your acting selfishly and being self-absorbed will only isolate and alienate your companion. Naturally, in the case of a relationship with God, it's more one-sided. You'll need more help from God than he needs from you. But certainly, he wants you to cooperate in his mission to reconcile the world to himself and bring all people into the loving communion of his family.

Actually, what we're talking about here is a life of prayer— prayer is how you chiefly communicate and relate to God. Essentially, prayer is relating on a personal level with God, so one of your tasks will be developing your children's prayer lives. Before you can do that, however, you need to establish your children's belief in a personal God and convey the possibility of a relationship with him. After all, to pray you have to believe there's someone who can hear your prayer and respond to your request.

REFLECT

Do you see God as personal or impersonal? Do you believe it's possible to have a relationship with God? Or do you think it's too informal or impertinent even to think about friendship with God? What's your fundamental stance toward him? Do you have a personal relationship with God?

PRAY

If you struggle with the concept of a personal relationship with God, take it to prayer. I know that sounds almost contradictory, but it can work. Ask him for the grace to believe in him as a person. Say, "God, if you really are personal, reveal yourself, and that side of you, to me." Then, don't be surprised when he shows up and does it!

LIVE

Once more, this step toward instilling lasting faith in your children will begin with you. Of course, you can't teach your children about a personal relationship with God or model one if you don't have one yourself. Regardless of how you've always thought of God, consider developing a relationship with him if you don't have one. I think you'll find it's worth it.

An excellent model for relationship with God is St. Thérèse of Lisieux. Her autobiography, *Story of a Soul*, depicts her bold, honest, childlike relationship with God. She knows with certainty that God is her Father. He is guiding her, looking out for her, and caring for her needs. She speaks her mind in prayer without holding anything back. The way she relates to him almost does sound irreverent, but it's the way a child speaks to the father she knows loves her. There are no pretenses. And, like a daughter, she wants to please him. He is the center of her life, and his will is paramount in her thoughts and actions.

St. Thérèse's attitude is theologically correct. Through our union with Christ, his relationship with the Father is our relationship as well. We really are sons and daughters of God in the Son. Therefore, we can relate to him as his children. Relationship with God is like any relationship. It means living with him, speaking with him, thinking about him in your daily life, going to him with problems, listening to his advice, considering him in everything you do, acting in ways that facilitate your relationship, and, in this way, loving him.

The Little Flower: The Story of St. Thérèse of the Child Jesus is an excellent book that presents St. Thérèse's story for children. I read this aloud to my kids in preparation for their First Communion. St. Thérèse could be the patron of First Communicants because her own preparation for the sacrament was incredible. She wanted to make her heart a beautiful garden for Jesus to enter and rest. It's a powerful witness and testament to her intimate relationship with God.

15.
PRAY FROM THE HEART

Relationship with God is fundamental, and it would be completely impossible without prayer. St. Teresa of Ávila, a great sixteenth-century Carmelite mystic who wrote extensively about prayer, said it was the entryway into the spiritual life. A relationship requires spending time interacting with someone, sharing thoughts, and exchanging ideas. That's what prayer is about.

For St. Teresa, prayer was effective only if it was a conversation. It wasn't enough to pray rote prayers like the Our Father and Hail Mary. They're not bad, just not enough—they don't encourage interaction with Jesus. They're not *relational* . . . and that's the key. In St. Teresa's opinion, if you said memorized prayers without thinking about what you were saying or whom you were speaking to, they brought no benefit at all.

HONESTY

What is relational prayer, and what kind of conversations do you have with God? It's not much different from the conversations you'd have in any relationship. In *God, Help Me: How to Grow in Prayer*, Jim Beckman outlines the two key "measures" for effective relational prayer—honesty and consistency. The honesty part seems like a no-brainer, right? Can you really lie to God? After all, he knows everything you're thinking. The problem is that we all have a large capacity for self-deception. God knows what's going on in your heart, but he wants you to be aware of it as well. God wants you to talk to him about your inner thoughts and feelings. For prayer to be effective, it has to be real.

When I first heard this, it was a revelation. I thought prayer had to be holy and righteous, with flowery language, to be good prayer. I didn't talk about certain things with God: the nasty, sinful things that tempted me and gave me secret pleasure. If I talked to God about those sinful temptations, then it meant I was that kind of person, and I didn't want to be.

However, I wasn't owning that sin—I thought that if I didn't acknowledge it, it somehow wasn't mine. Then I learned about honesty in prayer and got up the nerve to speak to God about all the sinful thoughts weighing on my mind. I think he breathed a sigh of relief and said, "Finally! Now I can start working with you." And he did! Things started happening that broke old shackles of shame and anger in my life. Honesty in prayer is not for God; it's for you. When you own what's in your heart—the raw, honest truth you're feeling—and relate it all to God, holding nothing back, he can start to change you.

CONSISTENCY

The second measure of prayer is consistency. You have to show up. How can you have a relationship with someone if you don't spend time with the person on a regular basis? You can't really, but that's the way we tend to operate with God. We go long periods without saying anything to him, waver in our commitment to him, and then give him a call only to ask for favors. And when we do talk to him, we hide our true feelings and our true selves by putting on a pseudo-holy mask. And we wonder why he doesn't seem to answer our prayers.

Consistency goes back to training in godliness. You have to make prayer a habit, a daily part of your life. Prayer is definitely like exercise in that regard. Just as one day of exercise doesn't do anything for you (except make you sore), one day of prayer won't change your life. Like exercise, prayer is only effective over the long term.

Consistency is a problem for many people, mostly because at first prayer seems boring. Remember, start small. If you have to, shoot for five minutes a day at first. Treat it like a daily conversation with your best friend. Talk about your problems, the things you're thinking and feeling, what's bothering you, what's keeping you up at night, and what's giving you joy. Relate to him your temptations, and tell him your desires . . . even if they're sinful. Bring it all out in the open. Tell him what you're grateful for as well. You don't want your time together to be just a gripe session.

Then, once you're done talking, listen. A conversation is a two-way street. Sometimes you'll get ideas, intuitions, and insights about the concerns you've brought to him. Other times you won't. However, I guarantee you'll always feel better afterward. The prayer habit may seem difficult at first, but eventually God will kick in and reward you with peace, consolation, and help. He won't be outdone in generosity, but you have to put your time in so he knows you're serious.

THE EXAMEN PRAYER

One form of prayer I've found helpful with my kids is the Ignatian Examen, which was developed by the soldier-saint Ignatius of Loyola, mentioned in chapter 6. This prayer is integral to his spirituality. It makes you aware of what's going on in your heart, what you should bring up with God in prayer, and how God is present and active in your life.

In the Examen, you reflect on the events of your day with an eye toward figuring out where God was influencing you. At every moment, God is actively working to guide you on a path toward himself. As he did with Israel in the desert, God is continuously leading us toward spiritual freedom. You just have to know how to listen. You feel God's influence in what St. Ignatius calls *consolation*—a feeling of comfort, security, love, happiness, and peace.

Similarly, influences from the evil spirit (which could be the devil, negative messages from society, or your own fallen human nature) are called *desolation* and are experienced as discord, uneasiness, irritability, and heaviness of heart. You have probably felt that sense of emptiness and pain in your chest when you've done something that you know is wrong or that you feel terrible about.

I did the Examen with my children every night before bed while they were in elementary school. I would have them think about what happened during the day and ask, "How's your heart? Is it joyful or heavy?" Asking this question helped my kids identify what they were feeling and what they wanted to talk to God about in prayer. The idea is that God's will lies in the things that give you consolation. You want to identify and do more of those things because that's God leading you. You want to move away from the things that give you desolation. That's the evil spirit leading you.

It took a while for them to understand the concept and figure out what to look for. At first the answer was always "I don't know." I had to help them get the idea of what to share, and I had to share my own high and low points as well. Slowly, they became able to think back over the day and recall their best and worst moments. The Examen often helped them recognize right from wrong and led them to better decisions.

ADORATION

Adoration introduces your kids to the sacred. It's just different in the church or chapel: quiet, calm, and holy. You can feel the presence of Jesus in the room. Adoration teaches kids reverence. Part of the secret to introducing kids to Catholicism is the example of other devout Catholic adults. Mass can be a mixed bag, but there's never a bad example at adoration. Everyone is reverent and respectful. Best of all, adoration is a prime place for encountering Christ. It's excellent relationship-building time because you are spending time in the physical presence of Jesus.

Adoration is the perfect time to introduce a little prayerful silence into your children's lives. Setting aside silent time is essential because it's in the silence that God speaks to us. Prayer is about conversation, and part of a conversation is listening. Silent time is especially important for kids because media is such a huge part of their lives. Television, radio, music, podcasts, and videos are all competing for attention. God can't break in if you're constantly bombarded with noise. However, when you unplug and are alone with your thoughts, God has the floor, and he can communicate his will for you.

I recommend having a time of family adoration. We worked this into our schedule for years and saw great rewards. You probably think I'm crazy to suggest you can get your kids to sit in silence and think about God. However, adoration is perfect for this. The space is already very quiet, and it's a semipublic place so it has a different feel from home. Kids will naturally be quieter there. I started taking my kids to adoration at a fairly early age, so I know it can be done. Here are some strategies.

We began taking our boys to the adoration chapel when they were toddlers, but we started small. Don't try to do too much right away. We would only stay ten, sometimes even five minutes at first, and we didn't go every week. If they made noise or got fidgety, we'd leave and try again another day. Then we worked our way up. I think dedicated adoration chapels work best because there are fewer distractions. However, sometimes a church can be good for active kids who like to wiggle.

The biggest question is *what do kids do at adoration*? Of course, it is a great time to pray and read the Bible. Gadgets are a great help. Using a Rosary app on a tablet or smartphone can be a major part of the adoration experience. There are also children's Bible apps with animations and sounds. Reading is a popular activity as well. That's what most people do at adoration anyway. It has to be spiritual reading, though. We used saint books and other children's devotions as well as children's Bibles.

When they were younger, we usually spent the last ten to fifteen minutes enjoying the silence with some hugs and affection. This is part of a larger strategy to make adoration full of "warm fuzzies." You want to associate positive feelings and emotions with going to church and doing church-y things. Hugs and cuddles are a huge part of that. What kid doesn't love getting that kind of attention from his or her parents?

REFLECT

What kind of prayer do you do? Is it conversational prayer or memorized prayers? Do you have a regular prayer time? Are you open to choosing one? Out of everything I suggest in this book, making time for prayer is one of the most important. Prayer is the essential spiritual practice and is crucial for growing in faith. It's also one of the most difficult things to do because it requires time alone, away from your kids and interruptions—often a rare luxury. It works best if you carve out an official time and schedule it on your calendar. Think of this as your appointment with God. It doesn't have to be a long meeting to pay huge benefits.

PRAY

What are your concerns about prayer? Are you worried about the time commitment? Are you hesitant about the honesty? Take a chance and talk to God about everything that's on your mind. Let him have it all, and don't hold anything back. Then sit quietly and listen for inspiration.

LIVE

The easiest time to pray with your kids is at bedtime. You want to slow them down and transition into a quiet and peaceful environment anyway. Do the Examen prayer with them, talk about their concerns, and then talk to God together and ask for his help. Eventually, they'll be able to do this on their own without your participation, but you'll have to teach them and model it at first.

Praying this way with your children has the secondary benefit of establishing you as a confidant and trusted advisor. This is an essential culture to create in your family. It will develop when you read the Bible with your kids and when you discuss faith with them in the ways we've talked about before. Getting down to the concrete applications of teachings will have that effect. However, there's a real bond that takes place when you pray together because you're sharing issues and walking through problems together. Open lines of communication like this are vital and you need to start early. Become a trusted source of comfort and guidance when your children are young so when they're teens and have real problems, they'll trust you and talk to you before making decisions.

If you want to delve into the Examen on an adult level, I recommend two books from Fr. Timothy Gallagher on Ignatian spirituality: *The Examen Prayer* and *The Discernment of Spirits*. They will definitely open your eyes and give you a new understanding of the spiritual life.

16.
STRUCTURE LIFE TO SUPPORT FAITH

This book is about change, about new attitudes, and radical commitments. I'm asking you to think differently about faith, religious education, and what it takes for Catholic parents to raise faith-filled children. You are the first and primary educators of your children. Ultimately, it's your responsibility—a pledge you took before God at their Baptisms—to teach them, nurture them, and guide them toward a full and active participation in God's life. You need to show them how to put faith into action.

It's clear that there's much more to raising faith-filled children than merely teaching them what the Church proposes. It's important, but it's only part of the equation. Children need adult examples in order to understand how faith is lived. They need mentoring relationships with close, trusted adults who can guide them. They must understand Catholic doctrine not simply in the abstract but as a unified whole that leads to a happy life and is oriented toward their salvation. Also, it's essential that they engage in practices that increase faith, have relationships that bolster faith, and live in an environment that cultivates faith.

Environment drives behavior. How our lives are structured influences how we act and what we do. Even our physical surroundings play a huge part in how effortless or complicated our choices are to live out. This is something only you can give your children—a life structured in such a way that faith is reinforced at every turn. If what they learn at the parish is not reinforced by the rest of their lives, there's little chance it will penetrate their hearts and translate into action.

WHAT DO YOU PUT FIRST?

One of the first things to consider regarding family environment is priorities. What do you value as a family? What do you reward? If you're too busy doing fun stuff on weekends to go to Mass, that sends a message. Not taking time for volunteer opportunities shows their level of importance. When participation in sports is valued far above religious education or church events, it communicates your family's priorities. Little things add up. Your children's adulthood will be built upon the foundation you lay. Once your children are out on their own, they'll most likely choose the same priorities you did.

It's long been my hypothesis, and Smith and Denton's research in *Soul Searching* bears it out, that faith-filled adolescents don't just fall into an active Christian lifestyle by accident. They are the way they are as teens because that's how they have been raised. Faith-filled families produce faith-filled teens. So it's essential that you make your home a place conducive to growth in faith, preferably from their early childhood. What do you want their lives to look like when they're on their own? Build that into your family life today. Do you want them to continue studying the faith? Study the faith now. Do you want them to be active in the life of the parish? Be active now. Would it be good if they volunteered? Volunteer now.

CATHOLIC FRIENDSHIPS

If you are your children's largest influence, who or what is second? Most likely it's their friends. We've all had significant friendships in our lives, maybe even friendships that changed our direction in life. Most often, an encounter with another person drives religious conversion. Friendships can be positive in that regard or negative. I think a monumental factor in my own distance from the Catholic Church as a teen came from the negative influence of my peers. I wanted to be popular and fit in. Being religious just didn't mix. My parents tried to steer me toward the parish youth group, but I refused. I wanted acceptance from a certain group of school friends and they weren't Catholic, therefore neither was I . . . or so I thought.

Acceptance is a driving factor in children's lives, especially as they get older. Often friends aren't chosen; our kids just fall into a group that accepts them. That can be dangerous if it's a group heading down the wrong path.

Go out of your way to set up interactions and friendships with Catholic peers. When my kids were in public elementary school, we got together with a group of Catholic families on a regular basis for play dates and socializing. Make connections with a Catholic Mom's group at your parish and cultivate friendships with like-minded families. This kind of contact has the added benefit of showing your children you're not the only family that is serious about living their Catholic faith. There are other families with the same values and making the same choices for their children.

Middle school and high school youth programs are a must. Your children need relationships with other Catholic kids, especially in high school. I'm not saying you have to make them go to youth group, but I am . . . sort of. I regret the adamant opposition I gave my parents regarding youth group. Who knows what could have happened in my faith life had I met and been accepted by

some Catholic friends . . . or even a Catholic girl who was into
God! Friendships are key. The direction of your children's faith life
will hang on the quality of their friendships.

MERGE SERVICE, FAMILY, AND SOCIAL TIME

Charitable work is a foundational religious practice. Service gets
you out of yourself and gets rid of selfishness. In chapter 7, I talked
about weeding your children's schedule of the urgent to make
room for the important. Well, this is the opposite. You need to find
space in your children's schedules for service. It's definitely an
"important."

Service, and/or ministry, makes faith bigger. That's just the way
it is. I became convinced of this when I started working for a parish and teaching. My faith and confidence in God grew exponen-
tially, and I've seen the same thing happen in countless others. It's
my conviction that no one can reach their full faith potential unless
they're involved in some ministry or service. It doesn't have to be
teaching. God has gifted everyone in different ways, but you have
to give back. God pours his love into us, and we're meant to make
a return of that love through service to others. As his love moves
through us, some of it stays and swells our souls in grace.

Smith and Denton found that teens who made time for church
activities merged them with other aspects of their lives. For these
teens, school, friendships, social time, volunteer work, and worship were all tightly knit together. You can blend family time and
church time, too, by doing volunteer activities together. When
your children are younger, participate in service projects as a family. I became a core team member in our older son's youth group,
making it a more of a parent-child activity. Shannon volunteered
to teach a religious education class on the same night our sons

were attending. A popular way of doing this is getting your kids involved in liturgical ministries such as altar server, choir, or lector. Here, your children engage in service while other members of the family attend Mass.

As your children get older, they'll be able to do church activities with friends, combining their social and religious lives. Of course, they will need reminders and gentle nudges to keep them going in the right direction, and that will fall to you.

KEEP A CATHOLIC HOME

Finally, consider the physical environment of your home. Is your house decorated with Catholic art and religious articles? It might seem trivial, but your physical environment has a huge influence on your attitudes and behaviors. Want to work out more and watch TV less? It actually helps to place your treadmill in a more convenient and accessible spot than your fifty-inch flat screen. Trying to lose weight by cutting between meal snacks? You'll have more success by tucking the Cheetos away in the pantry instead of keeping them out on the counter. Environment drives behavior.

In a similar way, if you want to think about God often, it helps to have holy reminders in plain sight all around the house. Sacred art, icons, statues, crucifixes, and the like are tangible signs of faith meant to keep you thinking about God and open to his promptings. God is continually showering you with grace that can help you make right judgments, think holy thoughts, and act godly. You're swimming in it. However, you need to be in the right frame of mind to receive it and act on it. Holy reminders keep God on your mind and dispose you to accept his grace. For the same reason, you should also give your children medals and/or crucifixes to wear, holy cards to keep, and statues to put in their rooms.

It doesn't have to be overt or gaudy. You don't need to hang a huge velvet picture of the Last Supper in your living room. I've seen many homes where Christian art and sculpture are integrated tastefully and simply exude the Catholic personality of that family. Even something as simple as crucifixes set above every door says a lot. Setting up an environment of faith like this solidifies the identity of the family in subtle but profound ways. It reinforces who your family is and what you believe.

One indispensable item for your Catholic home is a holy water font. In fact, you need several, which then leads you to the practice of blessing your children often. This is something I've done with my kids since they were toddlers. I blessed them with holy water every night as part of their bedtime ritual. I would trace the sign of the cross on their foreheads with holy water and say, "God bless you in the name of the Father, and the Son, and the Holy Spirit." Having a little font next to their beds reminded me every night. Then I put one by the front door and blessed them in the morning as they left for school. Sometimes we all blessed each other before going out.

As the spiritual leaders of the family, parents have the right to give blessings to their children. You are invoking God's protection and care on your spiritual charges. There are certain blessings reserved only for priests, but within the family a small blessing is fine. My kids have always loved it. They are teens now and still want holy water blessings before bed every night. I think it gives them a sense of security and a sign of loving care.

REFLECT

How do you structure your life to support your faith? What environmental changes will make growth in faith easier for you? Can you change your schedule to accommodate volunteer opportunities?

PRAY

In your prayer today, consider where the Lord is leading you to give your time and use your talent. Ask the Lord to lead you to ministries or volunteer groups in which you can best serve the Church and further God's kingdom.

LIVE

An engaging book on organizing family life is Patrick Lencioni's *Three Big Questions for a Frantic Family: A Leadership Fable about Restoring Sanity to the Most Important Organization in Your Life*. Lencioni is a *New York Times* best-selling business author and consultant, as well as a committed family man and devoted Catholic. His book applies some of the strategic business tools he uses with Fortune 500 companies to organize the confusion and craziness of everyday family life. Lencioni notes even business leaders who implement long term planning and goals at the office seldom work those out for their family . . . not to mention ordinary people who don't have a clue how to get started. He integrates business principles into developing a three-step plan for identifying what's important to your family and living it out. All of Lencioni's books are written in "parable" style, fictional stories that illustrate the points he wants to make, which makes for an easy and engaging read. Try out this book to identify and organize your family's "important" over "urgent" priorities.

17.
HELP YOUR CHILDREN MAKE AN ACT OF FAITH

We end as we began, considering faith—the faith your children need and are not getting from parish religious education programs alone; the faith you, more than anyone else, are perfectly suited to lead them to. I've laid out the type of education that promotes faith, the habits that grow faith, and the systems and structures that nurture faith. But again, how does faith work? How do you activate faith? How do you lead your children to make that personal act of faith that will set their lives on a course to follow God?

Faith is an elusive thing. There is no one set phrase or formula that will speak to the heart of everyone all the time. If that were true, there wouldn't be so many unbelievers. No, the paths to God are as varied as the differences in our personalities and life situations. But the Gospel is tried and true.

THE INVITATION TO ACCEPT THE GOSPEL

That God the Father created us out of love and wants more than anything to share his amazing life with us is a huge realization. Jesus endured horrible torture and died an agonizing death on the Cross to save us when we couldn't save ourselves. He sent the Holy Spirit to dwell in our souls, configuring us for relationship and divine union. Through Baptism, we are joined to Jesus and to his family, the Church. Here, in the sacramental liturgy, we are forgiven of sin and infused with divine life. God wants us to cooperate with his grace and be perfected in our humanity until we live ever more fully, ever more joyfully in him.

This is the Gospel, the Good News of whole, healed, and abundant life in Jesus Christ. God invites your children to share this life with him, but to receive its great benefits they have to want it and decide to accept it *verbally*. Many people downplay this last bit. They say it's not Catholic to require a verbal commitment to Jesus. But words are key. Words express the heart's intention. Baptisms aren't valid unless the priest says the words "I baptize you in the name of the Father, and of the Son, and of the Holy Spirit" while pouring the water. You aren't married until you give your verbal consent, saying "I do!" An act of faith in Jesus is not on the level of a sacrament, but words have power, and for this reason they need to be said.

In reality, young children aren't capable of making a decision that will affect the rest of their lives. What they say and think at age six will be long forgotten and even dismissed at fourteen or seventeen. This life decision for faith requires a series of commitments at certain moments in your children's lives. Each moment leads to progressively deeper commitment, which can then lead to a definitive commitment later in life. To activate your children's faith, you must take full advantage of these moments, which are actually milestones in a typical Catholic upbringing.

CATHOLIC MOMENTS OF VERBAL COMMITMENT

THE FIRST MOMENT: THE AGE OF REASON

The first moment of commitment comes at around age seven, the age of reason, when most kids make their First Communion. Belief in the Real Presence is a child's first act of faith, but preparation begins long before the First Communion year. You should start introducing your children to the story of salvation as soon as they're able to listen through Bible picture books. Equally important, introduce them to Jesus, the radiant center of God's plan. Your job is to lay the foundation for true religious feeling.

Every year on the anniversary of your children's Baptisms, light their baptismal candles and do a short ceremony to renew their baptismal promises, which are similar to the Apostles' Creed. The promises are included with the candles, but you can find them on the Internet as well. At their Baptisms, you professed faith for them, but by First Communion, they should speak the words themselves. This is a concrete act of faith and belief. Tell them God loves them immensely and wants to share his life with them through Holy Communion. Make sure they know that, in receiving the Eucharist, they are saying yes to a relationship with Jesus, a first yes that is meant to grow and develop. This is not a lifetime decision, but it's a serious commitment, one appropriate for their age that's meant to grow as they get older.

THE SECOND MOMENT: EARLY TEENS

The second moment of commitment is at around thirteen years old, the time most kids receive the Sacrament of Confirmation. The time between First Communion and Confirmation should be spent deepening their relationship with God. Greater participation in Mass, regular confessions, and frequent reception of the Eucharist, as well as a deeper understanding of the story of salvation, are crucial. You should also continue to have them renew their baptismal promises every year on the anniversary of their Baptisms. This way, they are making concrete acts of faith every year leading up to this big one.

During this time, children are becoming more self-aware and independent. They begin evaluating the world based on their own understanding and develop their own opinions. It's important that a Catholic worldview be solidified here. Confirmation is a significant milestone and the second opportunity for a formal, verbalized commitment to Christ. Your children should understand this as another level of relationship with God, an increase in baptismal graces resulting in a closer union to Christ and the Church. Their anointing at Confirmation also empowers them for mission in the Church. As they grow in faith, God will reveal more fully their unique mission. They aren't ready yet; they must be trained first. For now, their job is to continue to grow closer to Jesus and develop their relationship with him.

THE THIRD MOMENT: LATE TEENS

The third moment of commitment comes in the late teens, somewhere between sixteen and eighteen years old. Now they should take more responsibility for their faith. Not complete responsibility—they're still kids—but they need to be taught to think on their own because soon it will be all up to them.

At some point during this period, you should lead your children in a more formal commitment prayer to Jesus. They're making decisions now that set the tone for the rest of their lives. This isn't the last time they'll have to decide for Christ. There will be other moments all through their lives, but this is likely the last time you'll be able to lead them in a prayer like this.

SPEAKING THE ACT OF FAITH

So, if you lead them in a prayer, what should you say? Again, this is foreign territory for most Catholics because we don't ever do it. This is one area where we can learn from our Protestant brothers and sisters. They're often criticized for shallow faith because once you do an "altar call" or profess faith by praying the "Sinner's Prayer," you're set, but there's some wisdom to that practice. It's not the goal, but it's a good start, and psychologically, it's powerful for jump-starting faith.

Catholic religious education programs are vague about faith. They talk about it all day long, but they leave people hanging when it comes to the actual moment of decision. Leaving it up to the individual and hoping they "get the drift" doesn't work. You have to call people to take action, ask for a response, and lead them to a definitive decision for Christ. Am I saying that words make the difference? That without words there can be no decision, no commitment, no faith? Yes. Words are powerful. Words express intention. Words expressed truthfully from the heart can change your life.

Someone who fully understood this and didn't have any problem calling young people to action was Pope Benedict XVI. On August 21, 2011, at the concluding Mass of the World Youth Day in Madrid, he said this:

> Faith starts with God, who opens his heart to us and invites us to share in his own divine life. Faith does not simply provide information about who Christ is; rather, it entails a personal relationship with Christ, a surrender of our whole person, with all our understanding, will

and feelings, to God's self-revelation. So Jesus' question: "But who do you say that I am?" is ultimately a challenge to the disciples to make a personal decision in his regard. Faith in Christ and discipleship are strictly interconnected. And, since faith involves following the Master, it must become constantly stronger, deeper and more mature, to the extent that it leads to a closer and more intense relationship with Jesus.[1]

And then Pope Benedict directed Jesus's question to the gathered youth and provided the way to respond:

Dear young people, today Christ is asking you the same question which he asked the Apostles: "Who do you say that I am?" Respond to him with generosity and courage, as befits young hearts like your own. Say to him: "Jesus, I know that you are the Son of God, who have given your life for me. I want to follow you faithfully and to be led by your word. You know me and you love me. I place my trust in you and I put my whole life into your hands. I want you to be the power that strengthens me and the joy which never leaves me."[2]

This is a wonderful prayer to encourage an older teen to pray if he or she is uncomfortable making an act of faith in his or her own words.

This book is about creating the conditions that allow faith to grow. All of that is preparation. In the end, it comes down to asking your children, "Will you join me in living this beautiful life with God?" As anyone in business will tell you, if you don't ask for the sale, you won't get it. It comes down to the "ask"—delivered, of course, with a prayer that the Holy Spirit will speak to their hearts and they will listen.

You can do this!

NOTES

PREFACE

1. Center for Applied Research in the Apostolate, *Sacraments Today: Belief and Practice among U.S. Catholics* (Washington, DC: Georgetown University, 2008), 172.

2. John Paul II, *Familiaris Consortio*, "On the Role of the Christian Family in the Modern World" (Vatican City: Libreria Editrice Vaticana, 1981), 86, http://w2.vatican.va/content/john-paul-ii/en/apost_exhortations/documents/hf_jp-ii_exh_19811122_familiaris-consortio.html.

1. FAITH AT LAST

1. Pew Research Center, "Faith in Flux: Changes in Religious Affiliation in the U.S.," April 2009, revised February 2011, http://www.pewforum.org/2009/04/27/faith-in-flux/.

2. THE NECESSITY OF SAYING YES TO CHRIST

1. "Faith" in *Catechism of the Catholic Church*, 2nd ed. (Washington, DC: USCCB Publishing, 2000), 878–879.

3. THE POWER OF PERSONAL INFLUENCE

1. John Henry Newman, *Oxford University Sermons* (Westminster, MD: Christian Classics, 1966), 91–92.

2. John Henry Newman, *Historical Sketches III* (London: Longman, Green, 1903), 74.

3. John F. Crosby, *Personalist Papers* (Washington, DC: The Catholic University of America Press, 2004), 234.

4. FOUR WAYS PARENTS ARE ESSENTIAL FOR HANDING ON FAITH

1. Paul VI, *Gravissimum Educationis*, "Declaration on Christian Education"

(Vatican City: Libreria Editrice Vaticana, 1965), 3, http://www.vatican.va/archive/hist_councils/ii_vatican_council/documents/vat-ii_decl_19651028_gravissimum-educationis_en.html.

2. Paul VI, *Lumen Gentium*, Dogmatic Constitution on the Church (Vatican City: Libreria Editrice Vaticana, 1964), 11, http://www.vatican.va/archive/hist_councils/ii_vatican_council/documents/vat-ii_const_19641121_lumen-gentium_en.html.

3. John Paul II, *Familiaris Consortio*, 36.

4. Christian Smith and Melina Lundquist Denton, *Soul Searching: The Religious and Spiritual Lives of American Teenagers* (Oxford: Oxford University Press, 2009), 267.

5. Ibid.

6. Ibid.

7. Ibid., 27.

8. Pew Research Center, "Faith in Flux."

10. LEARNING THE STORY THROUGH THE BIBLE

1. Augustine, *The First Catechetical Instruction*, Ancient Christian Writers, trans. Joseph P. Christopher (Mahwah, NJ: Paulist Press, 1978), chap. 6, no. 10.

2. Ibid., chap. 4, no. 8.

13. TRAINING IN GODLINESS

1. Smith and Denton, *Soul Searching*, 269.

14. SEEK A PERSONAL RELATIONSHIP WITH GOD

1. Sherry A. Weddell, *Forming Intentional Disciples: The Path to Knowing and Following Jesus* (Huntington, IN: Our Sunday Visitor, 2012), 43.

2. Ibid., 44.

17. HELP YOUR CHILDREN MAKE AN ACT OF FAITH

1. Benedict XVI, *Words of the Holy Father at the Beginning of the Eucharistic Celebration*, August 21, 2011 (Vatican City: Libreria Editrice Vaticana, 2011), http://w2.vatican.va/content/benedict-xvi/en/homilies/2011/documents/hf_ben-xvi_hom_20110821_xxvi-gmg-madrid.html.

2. Ibid.

Marc Cardaronella is director of the Bishop Helmsing Institute for Faith Formation at the Diocese of Kansas City–St. Joseph, Missouri. He served as director of religious education at Holy Cross Catholic Church in Champaign, Illinois, from 2002 to 2014 and was a US Navy aviator from 1988 to 1999. Cardaronella grew up Catholic but stopped practicing his faith after eighth grade. After a series of what he calls "strange events," he was reintroduced to the faith of his youth and found meaning, purpose, and truth.

He has a bachelor's degree (with honors) in theology from Franciscan University of Steubenville, where he also earned a master's degree (summa cum laude) in theology and Christian ministry with a specialization in catechetics. Cardaronella and his wife, Shannon, have two sons and live in Kansas City.

AVE MARIA PRESS

Founded in 1865, Ave Maria Press,
a ministry of the Congregation of
Holy Cross, is a Catholic publishing
company that serves the spiritual and
formative needs of the Church and its
schools, institutions, and ministers;
Christian individuals and families; and
others seeking spiritual nourishment.

For a complete listing of titles from

Ave Maria Press

Sorin Books

Forest of Peace

Christian Classics

visit www.avemariapress.com

AVE MARIA PRESS
Notre Dame, IN
A Ministry of the United States Province of Holy Cross